AN UNENDING WAR

AN UNENDING WAR

A Memoir of Viet Nam

BOB GOFF

Library of Congress Control Number:		2017919254
ISBN:	Hardcover	978-1-5434-7312-4
	Softcover	978-1-5434-7313-1
	eBook	978-1-5434-7314-8

Print information available on the last page.

Rev. date: 12/21/2017

To order additional copies of this book, contact:
Xlibris
1-888-795-4274
www.Xlibris.com
Orders@Xlibris.com
761272

Dedicated to Sgt. James Ralph Snyder
All Gave Some, Some Gave All

Born July 16,1939 - Died June 27, 1967

Greater love hath no man than this, that a
man lay down his life for his friends.
—John 15:13–17

CHAPTER 1

My Father, Master Sgt. George W. Goff Sr.

F rom the time I was a young boy playing with plastic soldiers, I wanted to be a soldier just like my dad. Dad was a career soldier who stood six feet tall and weighed two hundred pounds. He looked exactly like you would expect an army sergeant to look, and he has influenced my life greatly. He always walked through the door commanding respect. Dad was mostly stationed in administrative positions except for his first four years in the military. He spent those initial years as a corpsman in the US Navy on the USS *Relief* off the coast of Okinawa during the invasion of the Japanese islands. Like most World War II vets, he didn't talk about the war. You would never know how it affected him except for seeing his eyes glisten as they teared up during an old war movie. It was a time when men were taught not to cry because it wasn't manly. Patriotism meant something then; *duty, honor,* and *country* weren't just words.

Father and son

My story is about a young infantryman's tour of duty in Vietnam. It is my story. I was there from April 1967 to April 1968. I was a recon sergeant with the Fourth Battalion, Ninth Infantry Regiment, Twenty-Fifth Infantry Division.

I was anxious to grow up and join the US Army, defend my country, and be a warrior. That was my dream, and I knew it early on. I was raised in a military family. My parents had three children, each spaced three years apart, me being the middle child, an older brother named George who was nicknamed Sonny, and a younger sister named Susan. We were raised in several states and spent three years on Okinawa, one of a group of islands belonging to Japan. It must have been there that I became so enthralled with the army way of life. We lived in military housing in an enclosed development with guards on the gates to prevent the locals from entering. Everyone who lived there was military or a dependent. All the kids would separate into groups and pretend to fight wars. I enjoyed playing soldier and exploring this island, which was the site of one of the main battles in the Pacific in WWII. It was common to find unexploded ordnance all over the place despite all the attempts to rid the island of these dangers. I can remember playing in our front yard with a toy dump truck at the age of six when I uncovered an unexploded bomb. I immediately left the front yard and informed my panic-stricken mother of this newfound treasure. She in turn contacted the EOD team (experts on demolition), which was stationed in the housing development, and they defused the bomb and removed it without any further trouble. All dependents were advised about unexploded ordnance and how to respond if they came across anything suspicious. As children we would explore the hillsides. On one occasion, we found a cave to explore and discovered a rusty old Japanese machine gun with rounds of ammo scattered around the floor of the cave. Of course we checked everything out before returning to report our find. It was a great time growing up. At seventeen, I was old enough to join the army, and I did. No more pretending. I signed up for combat arms. That's infantry, armor, or artillery; no desk job for me. My first assignment was basic training at Fort Knox, Kentucky. It was September 30, 1963, and Dad was stationed in southern Indiana. Vietnam was hardly mentioned, and advisors to the south Vietnamese were the only military that had been deployed there. War wasn't on my mind at this time, I just wanted to get through basic training. That was tough enough. Neither of my parents were happy about me enlisting, but I was starting to skip school and run with an ornery crowd. I'm sure Dad thought the discipline would do me some good. He would make the two-hour drive down periodically during those first eight weeks of my training—checking on me, no doubt—and it didn't hurt my relationship with the drill instructors when they saw Dad was one of them

Basic training is where we were taught the essentials of military life. You learn how to assemble and disassemble your M14 rifle and did it so often that you could do it in the dark—and did. The M14 weighed between ten and eleven pounds fully loaded and was much heavier than the .22s that I was used to. We went to the rifle range and learned to fire our weapons. Having learned to shoot as a young man while hunting with my uncle Albert gave me a step up on some of the others. Those treks through the woods with my uncle would provide me with a degree of comfort in my training and in the future to come. I was familiar with the sounds of the woods and how to navigate from one point to another. It was my uncle who taught me how to find my way in the woods should I become disoriented or lost. Simply find a stream and follow it, and it will eventually lead you to civilization. We also learned how to march and stay in step. By the end of basic training, we moved as one. We were taught hand-to-hand combat and stayed at it until we were proficient. We were taught about chemical, biological, and radiological warfare. We were given gas masks and sent through the gas chambers to test our wares against chlorine and tear gas, but we were not allowed to put them on until we had already breathed the gas. It was a lesson well learned. We had bayonet practice and learned that this was a last resort in the event we ran out of ammunition. We did push-ups, sit-ups, pull-ups, jumping jacks, and every other exercise you can imagine, and then we would run and run and run and run some more. In our classes, we learned the Uniform Code of Military Justice, the Geneva Conventions, the proper way to wear our uniforms, and even how to brush our teeth and sew on buttons. We were taught first aid and how to apply it to various wounds and injuries that we might encounter on the battlefield. We were taught how to read topographical maps and to use a compass so we could navigate over mountainous terrain or jungles. As fortune would have it, I became very proficient in these areas. While on field maneuvers, we learned the proper way to throw hand grenades. We would put everything we learned to use in the years to come.

Graduation day was soon upon us. Some of the men didn't make it. Some were sent back to repeat parts of basic, and some were sent home. I remember well that time when Dad was picking me up from basic and how proud I felt when I looked across the parade field, where we were standing in formation, and spotted him sitting in the bleachers behind the reviewing stand. He was wearing his dress blue uniform, and I think he was just as proud as I was. The military band started playing military march music—the kind that makes you stand a little taller and feel a little prouder. Our officers called us to attention and started us on the march around the parade ground, past the reviewing stand, and into the ranks of the US Army. I couldn't have been prouder.

Bob at graduation

By the middle of December, I was given a two-week leave, which meant I would be spending Christmas with the family. After that, I was on my way to Fort Gordon, Georgia, where I would spend the next eight weeks in advanced infantry training. At Gordon, we were taught how to fire mortars: the 81 mm mortar, the 4.2 mortar, and the 106 recoilless rifle, which is an anti-tank weapon. Learning to operate these weapon systems would differentiate me from the average infantryman and benefit me in the years to come. The average infantryman was a foot soldier, and I was trained on mortars and 106 recoilless rifles, which meant we were usually mechanized and didn't have to walk. An infantryman was a foot soldier and usually had to carry a sixty-pound pack on his back. Now that's a great advantage. Fort Gordon had an extensive escape-and-evasion course that we had to go through without being captured by the opposing force. This was a twenty-four-hour course that most of us tried to navigate at night. It was cold and miserable, but we made it through. At Fort Gordon, I got my first promotion and learned more about sand fleas than I ever wanted to know.

When we graduated from advanced infantry training, we were each assigned to a regular unit. I was going to Germany to join the First Battalion, Thirteenth Infantry Regiment, Eighth Infantry Division. I had five days to get to New York and aboard the USS *Patch* for an eight-day trip to Bremerhaven, Germany, and that was just enough time to swing by and say good-bye to the family before continuing my trip to the big city.

It was a cold March morning when I boarded the USS *Patch*. The pier was filled with family members and friends waving their last good-byes as a military band played and a tugboat assisted us in pulling away from the dock. We proceeded through New York harbor, passing the Statue of Liberty and watching as she disappeared on the horizon. I remember having a twinge of homesickness, but what the heck—I was living my dream of being a soldier.

The Atlantic Ocean was usually rough at that time of year, and it made no exception in our case. But this wasn't my first time to cross an ocean. When I was six years old, my siblings and my mother traveled from San Francisco to Okinawa on a twenty-one-day cruise to join my father, who was stationed there for three years. I was no novice when it came to traveling by ship. Before long, the sea was rolling, and large waves were breaking over the bow. A lot of men got seasick and were unable to eat. I was one of the fortunate ones, and eating didn't bother me at all. I'll say this—the food on board ship was some of the best food I had while in the military. The ship was an old troop ship used for transporting soldiers and had no resemblance to a passenger ship. Our sleeping assignments left a lot to be desired as we were billeted in the bottom of the ship and all the way back to the stern. You could hear the ocean rushing past and of course the unending noise of the propellers churning. It was not exactly a pleasure cruise. We played a lot of card games down in that hole as it was too cold and wet on deck. It helped to pass the days until we arrived in Germany.

It took seven days to reach the English Channel, and it felt good to see land again. We pulled into the pier at Bremerhaven, Germany, on the eighth day. It was snowing when we arrived, and we were loaded onto buses to be taken to the train station and begin the final leg to our destination: Baumholder. The ride to Baumholder took about seven hours, which was nice. It gave us an opportunity to enjoy the German villages and scenic countryside. Seeing the old villages with their quaint little houses and narrow cobblestone streets was like stepping back in time. The train was straight out of the last century and bore a strong resemblance to the old passenger cars that we saw in the movies. It was powered by an old steam locomotive, which required us to stop more than once to take on water. It was during these stops that we were first introduced to bratwurst sandwiches and German beer. How could you not love this?

We arrived in Baumholder at the end of the line. Seriously, they had to turn the train around to get back out. Once there, we were immediately processed and delivered to our respective units. My outfit was Headquarters Company, and I would be in the anti-tank platoon. Our barracks had once been the home of Hitler's Panzer division, with rooms that were furnished with three bunks, three lockers, and an old-fashioned coal-burning stove. We got a lot of exercise hauling coal up three flights of stairs and the ashes back down. The anti-tank platoon was equipped with what had been a French anti-tank missile called the ENTAC. It was about three feet long and housed in a metal container that served as its launch pad. The missile was guided by two wires trailing out the rear of the missile back to the launch pad and a connection to a joystick manned by the gunner. This weapon could pierce twenty-three inches of steel.

Preparing to fire the ENTAC anti-tank missile

We trained almost daily on a simulator that consisted of a small TV screen and a joystick; you would fire and then guide a small dot of light to a picture of the tank. That had to be the first computer game. It was high-tech back then. I was fortunate in mastering the system quickly and was placed in the position of gunner. Each team had two ammo bearers, one gunner, and one sergeant squad leader. Along with this new designation came a promotion to Specialist E-4. It was October 1964, and I had been in the army for fourteen months. We got to practice live fire twice while I was a gunner; I got lucky and was two for two. The ENTAC system was obsolete, and we ended up replacing it with the 106 recoilless rifle, which looks like a cannon mounted on a jeep, and it must be reloaded after each round. We were starting to hear more about Vietnam as occasionally we would hear of someone coming down on orders to go. Still, it wasn't a big deal, and I didn't give it a lot of thought.

Bob and Sgt. Robbins on a ten-day winter field exercise.

We were told that American forces in Germany were there as a deterrent to the Russians. We didn't have enough forces in theater to defeat them, only to hold them until reinforcements arrived. We had frequent drills and had to be dressed and in our vehicles within thirty minutes. We would then deploy to predetermined locations and wait for further orders. Normally we would return to base the same day, but in January 1965, we stayed out for a ten-day winter field problem. There was lots of snow and cold. Our unit had a proud history and was part of Gen. Patton's liberation force in World War II. They liberated the country of Luxembourg from the Nazis, and once a year, we would convoy to Ettelbruck, Luxembourg, and set up our equipment and displays for viewing by the people of Luxembourg. It was much like a county fair, and it was there that I met a young lady and her sister, Therese and Nicole Krippler. I would return to Ettelbruck as often as I could for the next year to visit Terry and her family. They put me up in a spare bedroom, and it was the first time I ever slept on a feather tick. It was good sleeping.

Bob in Luxembourg

Terry was a cute girl who was my age, and it didn't take long for us to become enamored with each other. She spoke three languages and graduated from the local Catholic high school. We would tour the streets of old Ettelbruck, walking together while she taught me about the history of the old castles and how her parents remembered being liberated by the American soldiers during the Nazi occupation. We often had lunch at the sidewalk cafes. She helped me to order from the menu, which was fine with me since I couldn't read a word on it. Besides, she had an accent that would melt your heart, and I was quite content to sit and listen. Saying good-bye was tough. I liked soldiering and took to it like a duck takes to water. I was promoted to Sergeant E-5 squad leader in August 1965, twenty-three months after I joined the army. I liked it so much that I reenlisted. After reenlisting, I was transferred back to Fort Knox, Kentucky, to push trainees through basic training. There was more talk of war. It was becoming more and more clear that we were in a conflict. It was while I was at Fort Knox that I started dating my high school sweetheart, Sue, again. We got married while I was stationed at Fort Knox.

Bob in Ft. Knox

I only stayed at Fort Knox for a couple of training cycles and requested a transfer to anywhere. I didn't care for the eighteen-hour days and thought there had to be something better. Around March of 1966, I was transferred to Dover Air Force Base in Delaware. I was assigned to the first US Army Escort Detachment. This is where they bring the casualties of war. The war hit home now, and we were seeing the horror, sadness, and finality of it all. The tragedy of it all was never more evident than my first assignment to escort the body of a nineteen-year-old Italian boy who was killed in action in South Vietnam home to his mother. The army mortuary service would prepare the body and make sure they had the proper uniforms, stripes, and medals for burial. Once the bodies were prepared for burial, they would assign a member of the escort detachment to accompany the body home. It was here that I began to understand what the real price of war was. I was a nineteen-year-old sergeant now and was just about to escort my first body home. The first was the most memorable. I was escorting a nineteen-year-old boy who was killed in action home to his mother. We were the same age. As best as I can remember, he lived in Eastern Pennsylvania. They had a military hearse drive us to the train station, where we placed the flag-draped casket on a wagon of sorts that was pulled by one of the train's employees alongside the train until we arrived at an empty freight car. I walked behind the coffin, making sure he was traveling feet first as tradition dictates. Together we placed the flag-draped coffin in the empty freight car, rendered a hand salute, and proceeded to the nearest passenger car. We were going home. We traveled through the night, and the next morning, I, along with employees of the rail company, removed the coffin and placed it on a gurney that the local funeral home had provided. Once again, I followed the flag-draped coffin and saluted as he was placed feet first into the hearse. I rode up front, and the funeral director informed me that the family would arrive about an hour after we got there. That gave him time to make sure the deceased was ready for viewing. Of course, he was. The military made sure of that.

The family arrived shortly after, and I introduced myself and told them that I would stay with their son through the funeral. We arranged for a military burial detail to do the honors as pallbearers and riflemen for his final salute. One musician would accompany the detail and play taps. I allowed the family time to spend alone with their son and assured them that I would take care of the arrangements and do whatever I could to assist them. After a while, they were ready to return home and invited me to accompany them, which I did. Home was just an average place in an average coal-mining town in Pennsylvania. The hospitality was anything but average. The dining room and kitchen were overflowing with food and drink brought in by friends and family. I sat with the boy's mother while she held my hand and told me all about this child she loved so deeply. I couldn't help but feel her pain as I tried to comfort her as best I could. When I was ready to leave for the night, she took my hand, placed it to her lips, kissing it softly, and said, "You smell just like my boy." I went to the motel for the night and got as much rest as I could. The next two days would be long ones. We made it through the viewings, the funeral detail had arrived, and I was informed by them that a major general from first army headquarters would be in attendance, along with some local politicians. Someone must have had connections.

On the day of the funeral, everything went with military precision. The detail was sharp in all their military splendor, the pastor gave a good sermon, the bugler played taps, and the riflemen fired three volleys to salute this fallen comrade. The pallbearers folded the flag very precisely, handed it over to me, stepped back one step, and saluted the flag. I proceeded with the flag to stand in front of where the young man's mother was sitting and started to present the flag by flipping it over to hand to her and said, "On behalf of the president 0f the United States and a grateful nation, I want ..."

Before I could proceed any further, she immediately fell to her knees, wrapped her arms around my legs, pulled me even closer, and said, "Will you be my little boy for a while?"

By this time, the tears were rolling down my cheeks, and I was doing my best to maintain a position of attention and proper military decorum. I was unable to finish my short speech; all I could say was, "Yes ma'am," as members of the family pulled her arms away and sat her back in the chair, apologizing to me at the same time. I placed her son's flag on her lap, smiled as best I could, and nodded my head as if to say, "Yes, I'll be your boy for a while."

I went back to attention, stepped back one step, and saluted. I walked off, trying to regain my composure. This was a time before I experienced the emotional numbing that would come with the experience of combat. I felt this mother's pain with every fiber of my body. I went back to the family home after the funeral to say my good-byes and grab a bite to eat before I left for Dover. It had been a hard day. When I went to check out, I was informed that my bill had already been paid.

The motel owner said, "Good luck, Sergeant," and I was on my way.

Two weeks later, my commanding officer called me in and read a letter commending me on a job well done. It was signed by Major General F. K. Mearns, First US Army. I continued to deliver bodies until late January 1967.

CHAPTER 2

On February 3, 1967, I was at our headquarters office in Dover, Delaware, when my first sergeant handed me a set of orders to deploy to the Republic of South Vietnam via APO San Francisco, California. He placed his hand on my shoulder and told me to go home and prepare my wife and informed me that I wouldn't be performing escort duty from this point on. I felt numb except for a hollow feeling in my stomach. I started the drive home, my head spinning and feeling lost. Someone had just pulled the rug out from under my feet. I tried to think rationally and start listing all the details I would have to take care of before I could relocate my wife back to Indiana.

I felt a lot of anxiety and was beginning to feel a little fear.

My heart sank, and a million thoughts raced through my head. At first, I thought about all the men I had buried and the families that had been left behind. I thought about all the riots and protests and the kids who were running to Canada to avoid the draft. Until now, the war seemed very far away. Now I would have to make some decisions. How do you tell your wife, your mom, your family and friends? I tried to clear my head and decided I would tell my wife first. She had witnessed the flag-draped coffins and wasn't any more prepared to hear this than I was. I returned home to a surprised wife. She wasn't expecting me until dinner. She knew something was wrong and asked what I was doing home.

I looked her in the eyes and said, "I've got orders to go to Nam."

We hugged and didn't say a word for what seemed an eternity. She stepped back with tears in her eyes and asked, "What are we going to do?"

I told her we would move her back to Indiana so she could be close to her family and friends. I took a couple days to consider everything and prepare myself for the inevitable. I thought about all the training I had received and convinced myself that I was as prepared as anybody else and that I would go and take my chances. It wasn't easy after taking all those bodies home. I wondered if my family would end up watching me come home in a body bag. The month of February was spent relocating my wife back to Southern Indiana and visiting my old friends I had gone to school with. Now I would have to go and see Mom and Dad, and none of this was easy. I'd already called to prepare them, but I don't think there's any way to prepare loved ones for this.

How do you say, "Hey, Mom, I'm going to war"?

It was difficult trying to reassure my wife and my mother that I would be okay. Mom started crying, and I was worried she might get me started. I tried to make light of it and joke about having to change my diet. After a while, she stopped crying and tried to be brave. Now we were both acting, and that's how we got through it. That night I could hear Mom sobbing in her bedroom. This just wasn't going to be easy. Dad just hung back and watched it all. He didn't say anything to me about it, and I didn't say anything about it to him; it wasn't necessary. We both knew what was ahead of me.

It was the first of March 1967 when I flew out of Pittsburgh on my way to California. Dad was kind of quiet as he hugged me for the last time. Mom and I hugged and said, "I love you," as did Sue and I. Both were fighting back tears. I promised to write. It felt awkward walking across the tarmac to the plane, leaving them huddled together, each with their own thoughts. There was nothing I could say to comfort them. I stopped at the top of the stairs, turned, and waved good-bye one last time. I knew they were probably wondering if we'd ever see each other again. That same thought had crossed my mind.

The flight to California was uneventful, except that you could see other soldiers scattered throughout the plane. Our short stay in California allowed the military to process everyone and give us our shots so we wouldn't catch some strange disease. Once we were processed, we boarded another flight to Vietnam, only it would stop in Anchorage, Alaska, first—of course it would. We were in short-sleeve shirts, and it was cold outside. Someone had a real sense of humor. We landed in Anchorage around midnight and deplaned while they were refueling. The terminal was empty and seemed much like a ghost town. It wasn't long before we were off again on the final leg of our trip. The long flight gave us an opportunity to become acquainted with each other. We were a real cross-section of America; most of the guys were enlisted men, with several sergeants included and a few young officers. All of us were going over as replacements for those coming home on normal rotation or those killed in action. The hours passed, and we were about to land. The plane grew eerily silent as we began to approach the runway. Nobody knew what to expect. We landed at Tan Son Knut air base just outside of Saigon. The door opened, and we started to deplane into an extremely hot and humid environment. Average temperatures ranged around 100°F and above, and the humidity was around 90 percent. One of the first things we noticed was how strange the air smelled, like wet bamboo or rotting vegetation. It's hard to describe. The sky was bright blue, and there was a lot of activity. Soldiers were coming and going in every direction, helicopters landed and took off, shuttles arrived at more than one waiting plane to take their passengers for processing. We were taken to a hangar, where we received an orientation as to what to expect in the next few days. We would be taken to another area on the other side of the base, where we would be issued jungle boots and fatigue uniforms, assigned a bunk, and attend an orientation on booby traps, Vietcong tactics, and a little on the Vietnamese culture. During this three-day period, they would have Vietnamese seamstresses prepare our uniforms by applying proper rank and name tags for a small fee.

While they were getting our gear ready, we attended the necessary classes on booby traps. Many of these booby traps are quite sophisticated, while others were rather simple but just as deadly. One of the more common booby traps was the punji pit, a hole in the ground approximately two feet deep with numerous sharpened bamboo stakes placed in the bottom of the pit and all around the sides pointing up. Not only were the stakes sharpened so they would impale your leg or foot, but they were also dipped in human excrement to ensure that you would get infected. I was in denial and didn't think anything was going to happen to me. I was just paying attention and going along for the ride.

Those few days would pass quickly, and little did we know how soon those lessons would be put to use. Our stay at Tan Son Nhut was kind of surreal. They had barracks, a post exchange (a store where you could buy anything), and mess halls just like a fort back in the States. Really, if it wasn't for the constant coming and going of the helicopters and the rumbling of artillery in the distance, you wouldn't know there was a war going on.

Mama-san carrying rice

I finally got my orders and would be moving out the following morning. I was assigned to the Twenty-Fifth Infantry Division at Cu Chi, a place that would become famous for the tunnels that ran under the base. These were said to have rooms large enough to be used as operating rooms and others that would accommodate patients, along with supplies and medicines for the Vietcong. There's a book titled *The Tunnels of Cu Chi* for those who are interested. The next morning, we were issued M-16 rifles and loaded on trucks for our trip to Cu Chi. We had a military police platoon providing security and leading the convoy. A large box of 7.62 ammunition was placed on each truck with instructions that we could load up if attacked. This didn't set well with the men being transported; after all, we were infantry and didn't like the idea of needing police protection. The trip from Tan Son Knut to Cu Chi was uneventful. Everything was new to us and exciting. The back of the truck had the canvas cover removed. This would allow us the opportunity to see Vietnam without the impediment of a canvas cover and allow us to return fire if fired upon. This was our first opportunity to witness the Vietnamese in their black pajamas and straw conical hats, the lush vegetation, the mud huts—some with thatched straw roofs, some with metal. I remember passing one little boy walking along the side of the road holding three or four huge dead rats by the tail. When I asked what he was doing with dead rats, one of the MPs replied that it was probably dinner. It was a long, bumpy ride, and I was glad when we arrived in Cu Chi. We discovered that it was a good-sized town with a sprawling military encampment nearby, which was going to be our new home.

Local children

As we unloaded, they started separating us by units. My name was called, and I was assigned to recon platoon, Headquarters Company, Fourth Battalion, Ninth Infantry Regiment. We were named the Manchus, an honorary title given to the Fourth Battalion, Ninth Infantry for exemplary performance when it became the first unit to break into the Forbidden City. After the fall of Peking, China, legend has it that a sentry of the Ninth Regiment remained on guard at the entrance of the Forbidden City for almost one year until the regiment was withdrawn in mid-1901. The history of this unit dates to when it first came into existence in January 1799, in Maryland. The unit had distinguished itself during the war of 1812 and fought in the Mexican war in 1847 and 1848. In 1855 the unit was transferred to the western front and returned to take its place during the Civil War and fought in places such as Chickamauga, and Murfreesboro to name just a couple. No less than four hundred skirmishes were fought with numerous Indian tribes led by great war chiefs such as Geronimo, Crazy Horse, and Sitting Bull. The list goes on and on. It was easy for an impressionable young man such as myself to feel a great sense of pride as a member of a unit with such a prestigious history. There was a Sgt. Jim Snyder who was waiting to take me to my new company. He greeted me with a winning smile and a firm handshake, and immediately I knew I was going to like this lanky, good-natured guy.

Jim was in the same platoon and took me on a quick tour of the compound. He informed me that he was from Pennsylvania and that he already had eight months under his belt. He became a very close friend and mentor. When we arrived at our platoon, he began introducing me to the men. As we shook hands, I overheard one of the men say, "Another FNG." (I had no idea what an FNG was, but I wasn't going to show my ignorance in front of everyone.) After the introductions, we proceeded to the company headquarters, where I officially reported in. I was introduced to a young lieutenant who headed up recon. He told Jim to get me settled in and then we'd talk.

Jim and I walked over to the twenty-man tents, which would become home when we weren't in the field. Each tent was surrounded by sandbags stacked about three feet high. This was to protect the men from mortars and rockets that the Vietcong would fire at our compound. They had wooden walkways made from pallets that went between each tent to the showers, mess tent, and outhouses. The walkways were an attempt to keep us out of the mud during monsoon season that would start in August and last two or three months.

After settling in, Jim, Sgt. McDonald, Sgt. Foster, and I sat down with the lieutenant and began to reorganize the squads. Jim and I shared a tent with the men in our squads. Each squad would have twelve men if they were at full strength, which they never were. The number of men would fluctuate all the time due to normal rotation back home and casualties suffered. Each of us had three jeeps assigned to us, one with a .50-caliber machine gun, one with an M-60 machine gun, and one with a 106 recoilless rifle, which is an antitank weapon but also has an anti-personnel round. The anti-personnel round can be set to explode at a distance determined by the gunner and explodes, emitting thousands of steel shards. In the beginning, I would have ten men directly under me. This would change if the task at hand required more than one squad. If more than one squad was required, the ranking sergeant would be in charge. Our rankings were determined by the date of our promotion to sergeant; Jim was senior, then me, then Foster, and then McDonald.

I said to the guys, "By the way, earlier today I heard the term FNG. What does it mean?"

They laughed and said, "**expletive deleted** new guy. Nobody wants to know your name, or get too close because FNGs have a high mortality rate." I learned a bit later that the life expectancy of an infantryman in a firefight was less than a minute. They sure don't put that on the enlistment posters.

After our meeting, I met with my squad and picked Dave B. to be my driver and radio operator. Dave was from Washington, Indiana, about thirty miles from where I went to high school in Bedford, Indiana. I spent the rest of the day getting to know my guys; they were a pretty good bunch. I was starting to feel better about the whole thing. Jim Snyder had a road sweep in the morning and invited me along so I could familiarize myself with the mine sweeping of the roads. I jumped at the chance. It didn't take long before we came upon a suspicious reading on the mine detector. Jim grabbed my arm and said, "C'mon, I'll show you what this is all about." As we approached the man with the sweeper, Jim was telling me everything to look for: potential secondary booby traps, usually located off to the side of the road, or possible ambushes to coincide with the explosion of the primary explosion. He was full of interesting little tips, some that were never taught in training and could only be learned by experience. He asked if I knew how to check for a mine.

I said, "Yes. Do you want me to do this one?"

He replied, "If you feel comfortable, give me your rifle to hold and have at it."

I retrieved my bayonet from my scabbard and started crawling toward the suspected mine, checking the soil on my way to make sure it wasn't disturbed. I was a little nervous, I began probing with my bayonet around the spot until I hit something hard. By this time my heart was racing. I signaled Snyder to move back and slowly started removing the soil from around and off the object. It didn't take long to realize it was just a piece of scrap metal. Thank God. I removed it after making sure there wasn't anything under it, and we mounted up and proceeded with the sweep. Jim told me that the Vietcong would test us by placing scrap metal in the road, and as soon as we got careless, they would plant the real thing. Planting duds was also a cheap way of delaying allied convoys. The rest of our trip was uneventful, and we returned to base.

Bob and Jim disarming booby trap

The procedure for mine removal was changed a few weeks later. Instead of probing for the mine with a bayonet, we simply placed a quarter pound of C-4 (plastic explosive) on top of the suspected mine and blew it in place. This change was much safer and saved time.

We had various assignments besides minesweeping details. At times, we would escort medical personnel to rural villages to immunize the children and attend to the sick. This was a typical civil affairs action and was used quite frequently to win the hearts and minds of the local populace. We also provided heavy weapons support for our base camps perimeter. Another duty in which I was frequently involved was ambush patrols.

These would be conducted at night by moving on foot to a designated location anywhere from two thousand to three thousand meters outside of base camp. We would set up an ambush along a trail or road and wait for the Vietcong to walk into our kill zone before taking them out.

The next week I began taking over the mine-sweeping detail from base camp to Go Dau Ha. While sweeping the roads, we would also provide security for the supply truck that was carrying laundry to mama-sans. *Mama-san* was the term you used to show respect to women of age with no distinction as to marital status. This was a Vietnamese woman who had contracted with our outfit to do the laundry on a weekly basis. She also had many young ladies who would entertain the troops for two hundred piasters apiece, no pun intended. That's two dollars American money. I know there are those who would find this distasteful, but this is part of war. These men had fought and watched friends die; some had suffered wounds themselves, some seen and some unseen. Mama-sans was a place where the men looked forward to going to forget about the war, the killing, the maiming, and the dehumanization of people.

Bob center background waiting for convoy at mama-san's

We would usually wait at mama-san's until a supply convoy would arrive and then escort the convoy back to base camp. We couldn't afford to get careless with security, so we would leave one man on each gun while the rest of the men relaxed—at least momentarily, anyway. Play time was over for the men, as word came over the radio, "Convoy ten minutes out. Everybody get it together, mount up." The convoy arrived, and we assumed control and escorted the supply vehicles to base camp, waving good-bye to the locals and hello to what we were there for.

When we got back from mama-san's, it was already afternoon and we were told recon had to send out a twelve-man patrol that night, and I was the man who had to take it. This is my first night ambush patrol. This is where all your training over the years comes to fruition. Jim Snyder came by and gave me some more pointers about the patrol for the night.

The mission was to depart base camp at dusk with twelve men and proceed on foot to a designated location beside a road leading into a local village. Once there, we were to set up an ambush and execute it when enemy entered the kill zone. Minus action, we would remain in that position until dawn. At dawn we would return to base camp using an alternate route. Upon arrival, we would throw a smoke grenade into the clearing and identify ourselves to the men on the perimeter. I would depart base at dusk with twelve men.

CHAPTER 3

We grabbed a few hours of sleep, and then I had to inspect the patrol. It was necessary to make sure weapons were clean and that everyone had enough individual ammunition. I had to assign ammo bearers to assist with ammo for the machine guns and make sure mosquito repellent was available.

Everyone had to take their malaria pills for the day. I would be compass man and pick a pace man (He determines how far you've gone by measuring his normal pace and computing his number of paces into a hundred meters. He then ties a knot in a cord or rope every hundred meters. Twenty knots equal two thousand meters.). Next, I had to pick a point man. He was the one who walked in front of a patrol to detect an ambush or anything out of the ordinary. My driver, Dave B., would operate the radio. I needed to pick a second-in-command, in case I would become incapacitated, and make sure everyone knew who it was and what our mission was. Each man would be issued two hand grenades, and the team would carry a total of six Claymore mines. The M18 Claymore is a directional fragmentation mine that is eight and a half inches long, one and three-eighths inches wide, and three and a quarter inches high and weighs three and a half pounds. It contains seven hundred steel balls and has one and half pounds of C-4 plastic explosive that is initiated by a number-two electric blasting cap. In this situation, it would be used to initiate the ambush or to defend our position against attack. The Claymore has a fifty-meter kill zone. It can be detonated by squeezing the firing mechanism two times, which generates an electrical charge, or by setting a trip wire and letting the enemy detonate it. They are moderately effective up to one hundred meters and dangerous out to 250 meters. All canteens had to be full. A full canteen won't make noise by sloshing water around. Everyone was to have a first-aid packet and poncho. These were most of the details you checked, as I remember them. I'm sure I've forgotten some. Oh yeah, bring toilet paper just in case.

It was dusk, time to move out, everybody lock and load. Jim saw me off at the wire, and said, "I'll see you in the morning, Goff, right?"

"Right," I replied.

I knew he was concerned and with good reason. We had been receiving harassing fire and some mortar rounds at night. Somebody was out there. We slipped through a break in the wire and heard them closing it behind us. We only had to go about 150 yards before we entered the wood line. Everyone was quiet as we got underway. The woods were thick but there was not a lot of undergrowth—a good thing. It was important that we didn't make a lot of noise. We would proceed for the two thousand meters, and the road was just off to our left. As we came out of the wood line, I saw approximately ten lights out to my front varying from three hundred to four hundred meters away, and they were moving. There were rice paddies in front of me and across the road. They were dry that time of year as the monsoons wouldn't start until August. The locals were under a dusk-to-dawn curfew, so there shouldn't have been anybody out there. There was no logical explanation for the lights. I'd heard that the NVA were so bold that they were driving trucks down the Ho Chi Minh trail with their lights on if they weren't currently threatened by air power, it wasn't unusual for ground forces to use flashlights to see the ground in front of them. I really didn't know what the lights were for, and I wasn't going to take any chances. I did know that everyone was under curfew, and anybody who was out was pretty much fair game. My blood was racing, as well as my mind. I gave the order to set up a hasty ambush and do it quietly. We had two M-60 machine guns, so I placed one on each of my flanks. I radioed in to the tactical operator and reported my sightings. He wanted to know if they had weapons. Just my luck—my first patrol and I got a second lieutenant in the tactical operations center. Real comforting!

"Sir, I can't see if they have weapons. It's dark, nighttime."

He replied, "Don't fire until you see weapons."

Now, this politically correct son of a bitch was starting to get on my nerves. "There's a curfew out here, sir." That meant that anybody who was out there was fair game.

His reply was the same: "Don't fire until you see weapons."

By that time, the lights were moving around. My imagination started running wild, and I was wondering if they were point men for some Vietcong regiment. There was nothing that explained those lights at night. I was scared. I thought they knew we were there and were possibly trying to encircle our position. I had to take a leak but I was so scared I didn't dare show it. So, I unbuttoned my fly, got on my knees, trying not to be detected, and tried relieving myself across the rice paddy dike. It didn't take long to realize I needed more elevation. Now that was no laughing matter. I was trying to stay low enough so as not to be seen. I finally got done, but I left my fly unbuttoned just in case I had to go again. The tension was so thick that you could cut it with a knife. The men kept looking at me and waiting for me to make a call. Everybody was scared. That was normal. I was in charge, and I needed to portray confidence. It was dark as it could be, but the moon was just starting to appear in the night sky. That might help.

Silently, I began to pray. "God, I need your help. It looks like we're going to be in it pretty deep. I don't know what's going to happen, but I pray that you'll watch over my men and get them back safe. God please, if somebody has to die, let it be me. Please, please get my men back safe, and if I'm to die, forgive me."

I continued talking to the tactical operation center, my voice barely above a whisper and requested to speak to someone senior to this lieutenant. I was told there was no one around. Then, I heard over the radio a call to the tactical operations center.

"Manchu six, this is bravo six." Manchu six was the call sign for the Battalion Commander, and bravo six was the call sign for B company's commander, a captain. "I can assist recon," said the Bravo commander over the radio. "I can be there within the hour with a full platoon."

"Negative, Manchu bravo six," was the reply that came back from the lieutenant.

I passed the word down the line that we were on our own. Things weren't getting any better, and I still had to relieve myself. Suddenly, after what seemed a lifetime, my radio operator, Dave B., elbowed me in the ribs; someone was coming down the road. I called the tactical operations center and said, "We've got one coming down the road."

He replied, "Wait till you see weapons."

I had to decide. I couldn't see any weapons and he'd already passed half of my men, and not a soul moved. Damn, these guys were disciplined. I loved it. He was entering my kill zone. I laid the mike down and squeezed the trigger on the claymore. Click, click, click. Nothing. I took my rifle and started sighting in on this guy's head and began to squeeze the trigger ever so slightly just like you're taught. All of this was only taking milliseconds. As all this was taking place, a full moon started rising into the sky, and it was silhouetting the man coming into my kill zone.

"Screw that damn lieutenant!"

All of a sudden, a voice entered my mind: "Thou shalt not kill."

I was still squeezing, but I glanced quickly at my radio operator to see if he heard anything. His face was expressionless. He hadn't heard anything. He was fixated on the target. It must have been my imagination. I continued to squeeze the trigger and once again. "Thou shalt not kill." This time it seemed a little louder. I continued to squeeze the trigger but began to raise my rifle ever so slightly. *Boom!* I swear I saw his hair part as he dove for the rice paddy. It was an intentional miss. Everyone else started firing, and the lights went out. The firing continued for about a minute. We weren't receiving any return fire, so I called for a cease-fire. Suddenly everything was quiet, except the radio. They wanted to know what was going on. Come to find out that when I put the mike down, my radio operator accidently keyed the mike and they heard everything from, "Screw that damn lieutenant" on. Nobody ever said a word. The tactical operations center called and asked if I was receiving any fire and if I had a body count. I simply replied no. I couldn't help but wonder which of us God was looking out for—the target or me, or maybe both. We did pull back and set up a defensive position, but everyone was too excited to go to sleep, so we waited until dawn and started back.

The sky was still turning gray when I called in and said, "I'm throwing smoke."

They came back, "It's green."

"Confirmed, I'm coming in." The reason we throw smoke when we're coming in was to make sure everyone knew it was us. Enemy forces had been known to try and sneak in pretending they were friendly.

The men headed for showers and chow while I discussed the night's events with Sgt. Snyder. Another team was sweeping the road, so it was a good time for rest. The sergeant major had called recon and wanted to see me. He had gone to the ambush site and nearby village to find out what they knew about the previous evening. The lights turned out to be South Vietnamese soldiers violating curfew and hunting frogs outside their compound. The sergeant major said they were damn lucky we didn't kill someone. If he only knew ... One guy was real lucky or very blessed. One thing I knew for sure—God was sending me a message.

Headquarters sent a runner down to recon platoon informing us that we would have to furnish headquarters with a twelve-man squad to accompany them on a battalion-sized search-and-destroy mission in the Michelin rubber plantation the next day. I got the assignment. We were going to be inserted the next morning by helicopter. The next morning, we formed up with the headquarters group to load up and head out. We had three-line companies consisting of approximately six hundred men and roughly twenty-five in the headquarters group. We loaded up on the Hueys and headed for the plantation. It was a good twenty-minute ride before we hit the ground. The line companies landed first and secured the landing zone (LZ). It was a cold LZ. Once we arrived, everyone started spreading out, and my squad formed up with the brass and provided them with security. We began our sweep into the plantation, and it was easy to see that it had been a beautiful place at one time. We hadn't been there thirty minutes when we heard aircraft flying overhead. They were spraying agent orange, a defoliant used to kill the vegetation and deprive the enemy of its hiding places. Somebody screwed up in logistics because it wasn't long before we could see it dripping from the trees. Our battalion commander was hot on the radio, and our battalion executive officer was instructing everyone not to touch anything and start back to the LZ. That spray was dripping all over the place, even on the men. Soon after, the choppers were landing and we were leaving. We heard that the planes were flying out of Tan Son Knut, which turned out to be the busiest airport in the world during the mid-'60s. It was also the center of the military's defoliation program. Between 1962 and 1971, the US military sprayed over twenty million gallons of defoliants to rid the countryside of vegetation that would enable the enemy to hide. These defoliants are more commonly known as agent orange. There were over four thousand spraying missions flown during my tour in 1967 and 1968 alone, dropping a total of ten million gallons. A large portion of this occurred where my division was operating. There are numerous diseases that are attributed to the exposure of agent orange, and it has had a devastating impact on the men and women who served in Vietnam. My brother Sonny wound up being a victim of agent orange. He deployed to Vietnam in 1969 and was diagnosed with lymphoma (brain cancer) in March of 2016. He died six months later. My brother was a captain, a pilot, and highly decorated for the numerous missions he flew in support of ground operations. He went on to serve a full twenty years before retiring as a major in the US Army. We miss him greatly but thank God for the time we had together.

We pretty much followed the same routine through April and May except that the Vietcong had started mortaring us at night on a regular basis. Sometimes it was safer on patrol—safer but not necessarily more comfortable. When you go on patrol, you carry a full load of ammo, two hand grenades, and possibly some of the ammo for the machine gun, a couple of parachute flares, first-aid kit, canteen, web gear, steel helmet or boonie hat, poncho and poncho liner, flashlight with red lens, smoke grenades, c-rations, map, compass, mosquito repellent, rifle, and probably fifty to sixty pounds on a patrol like this. You would pack more if you were going for a long-range patrol.

We would leave at dusk. The temperature was still hot, in the eighties to nineties. We put mosquito repellent on our hands, faces, and necks and wore long sleeves to protect our arms. We would begin to sweat as we moved through the jungle; the repellent would start running down our faces and into our eyes, burning like crazy. We would keep wiping our faces, but we were wiping off the repellant along with our sweat.

We finally arrived at our location and settled in for the night, always on guard, eyes burning, straining to see something out there. We listened quietly, hoping we wouldn't hear anything. Then we heard the mosquitoes as they started swarming around our ears; we wanted to slap them, but we couldn't. Sound travels; they might hear us. We would apply more repellent and then start sweating again. We couldn't go to sleep because we might snore. We sat there waiting and waiting for an elusive enemy to come along. "Stay alert, don't fall asleep. Hopefully dawn will come soon," I said to myself.

After a very stressful night finally began to pass, we started hearing birds as they awoke. The sky turned gray, and we realized we had lived to see another day. We checked our surroundings, making sure no one had moved in on us. The bushes all still looked the same; I guessed we were okay. I would gather my men and start back, but I didn't go the same way. If we did, they might have seen us and be waiting for us to come back. We came to a clear field, so we stopped, knelt, and scoped out the wood line across the clearing. Nothing was moving.

"Damn!" My leg was burning like fire; I had knelt down in a nest of fire ants. I couldn't make too much noise, but they were biting right through my pants. We had to move cautiously. I sent two men across, and they made it without incident. We followed two at a time, always on guard.

Finally, we got back, called in, and told them we were approaching. They wanted us to throw smoke, so we did. They came back, "It's green. Come on in."

We replied, "Affirmative."

One of the men on the wire inquired, "Did you have a good night, Sarge?"

"Yeah, it was quiet," I said.

I stopped in to see the medic. My knee was now swollen, and I had bites up and down my leg. They smiled like it was a joke and gave me some lotion to stop the itching and burning. The swelling would go down in time.

Our bunker in Tay Ninh

During my time with recon, I personally led at least two dozen ambush patrols. Most were uneventful. However, there were a couple where we executed the ambush and killed a total of six of the enemy. The most memorable for me was an ambush which we initiated when three Vietcong guerillas carrying booby traps entered our ambush site from our left flank. When they advanced to the center of our kill zone, we opened fire. They never knew we were there. They dove for cover, but it was too late. Two of them were shot before they hit the ground. The third one tried to return fire, but he too was hit before he could get off a good shot. We quickly gathered up their weapons and booby traps and pulled back to an alternate site. This was done because our position was now compromised, and we didn't want to take any chances. We were fortunate and did not suffer any casualties of our own. Somebody else would take care of the bodies the next day.

The month of June rolled around, and the rumor mill was really cranking up. The word we got was that our brigade would be moving to Tay Ninh within weeks. Tay Ninh is located next to the iron triangle and much closer to the border of Cambodia; both are known enemy sanctuaries. The Ho Chi Minh trail is a major resupply route for the North Vietnamese Army. Lately the North Vietnamese had been shipping men and supplies down the trail and into III Corps, which was our turf.

We were preparing for our upcoming move when our platoon leader, a young lieutenant, was told to sweep our perimeter the next day for booby traps. Intel had reported Vietcong setting mines in the area. I was supposed to grab a chopper and head to Tan Son Knut for an opportunity to call home. We had to use a series of ham operators and phone operators to get a call through. We didn't get the chance often, and now I was going to miss my chance because the lieutenant wanted me to go with him on patrol. Sgt. Snyder went to the lieutenant and suggested he take the patrol so I could make my call. I had been leading most of our foot patrols and wasn't surprised that I was picked for this one too.

Sgt. Snyder came to me and said he already talked to the lieutenant and that he was taking my place and for me to go ahead with my scheduled call home. I said no at first because Jim was getting to be a short-timer, due to return home in July. It was custom to keep short timers inside the wire so they wouldn't get killed or hurt when they were so close to going home. He wouldn't hear of it and reminded me that I had been leading more than my share of patrols. Jim said he was getting bored staying in camp. So on the morning of June 27, Jim and I shared breakfast and talked about the day ahead. I hitched a helicopter ride back to Tan Son Knut, while Jim prepared the men for a sweep of the perimeter for booby traps. I made my call and was back at the helipad hitching a flight back to base when we heard over the radio that recon platoon had casualties from a booby trap. My stomach was in my throat as they were being medevac'd to Tan Son Knut. I made my way over to the hospital's landing pad, anxious as to what I was about to experience.

We had two ships, and the first was wounded men—four of them. The floor of the chopper was red with blood. One of them told me it had been a Chinese claymore. I was sick to see members of my platoon coming in that way. The second chopper was about to land, and I was heartbroken to think about what I might find on it. I made my way over, only to find the lieutenant and my good friend Jim Snyder had both been killed.

I was more than stunned and asked God, "Why him and not me?"

It didn't make any sense. I was grief-stricken to find that my best friend had been killed. I wanted to scream, and I wanted revenge. The army listed his cause of death as multiple fragmentation, which would be consistent with a Chinese claymore mine. My best friend and mentor had died in my place, and I was sick and feeling a whole lot of guilt. When in camp, he was the first person I would see in the morning and the last at night. Jim had taught me how to stay alive. I was going to miss him and his witty sense of humor. I know now that the best tribute I can pay to Jim is to live my life and make the most of it. But I still feel survivor's guilt and wonder why he died and not me. There was no time to mourn as I had to lead a patrol the next morning to sweep the road for land mines.

It's forty-six years later, and I still tear up when I think of this man and the sacrifice he made for me, and I still feel the guilt.

Jim was buried at home in Pennsylvania, and his wife wrote to thank us for the flowers and kind thoughts. He had spoken of us often in his letters. I saved her thank-you note and have it to this day. I called and talked with her a couple of times after I returned stateside. She knows how to contact me if she ever needs help.

Sgt. James Snyder

The red blooms are called
anthuriums. Jim & I saw
many of these while he
was on R & R to Honolulu in
March.

Phyllis Snyder

Thank You All

Phyllis Snyder

I am enclosing some
pictures of the wreath
so that you may see
what you purchased.
Again I thank you
from the bottom of my
heart.

Sincerely,
Phyllis Snyder

A Brownie Creation

RUST CRAFT

598X442-1C

It is the lifted face
that feels
The shining
of the Sun.

H.B.S.

CHAPTER 4

It was July 1, and we were leaving Cu Chi and heading for Tay Ninh. The recon platoon was leading the way, with the rest of our jeeps spaced intermittently throughout the convoy for security. We received a new platoon sergeant before we left. He was an older guy, late thirties, who looked as though he was late for his retirement. I didn't think he would be going out on patrols though. Still he was a nice guy.

Bob with convoy

When we arrived at Tay Ninh, we set up camp in a clearing a few miles from Trang Bang. (That's its real name.) We started building our base camp from scratch. I couldn't begin to guess how many sandbags we filled to build our bunkers, but it was a bunch. The locals got as close as they could to watch and marvel at the helicopters, as they brought sling after sling of building materials—mostly sandbags and some perforated metal sheeting that was used for building airstrips. We used it as roof supports to carry the weight of the sandbags we placed on top of our bunkers. Several flights had brought

Constantine wire to string around the perimeter. Jim taught us how to tie empty beer and soda cans together and tie them to the Constantine wire. When anybody tried to sneak into your perimeter, they acted like wind chimes and alerted the troops.

Bob and guys building bunker

We still had to sweep the roads from our base to the town of Trang Bang and then to Charlie Company and back to Trang Bang. Charlie Company was a small outpost with just one infantry company. Usually they had around two hundred men but were getting along with about a hundred fifty. It was only about three miles as the crow flies from our base camp to Charlie Company. To get to either of these camps, one had to go through Trang Bang. That added another four miles, and that was where the road divided. One went to Charlie Company and the other to our base camp. It was simply a triangle, and that triangle was heavily wooded and about three miles wide at the widest spot.

Sweeping the road from base camp to Trang Bang was about four or five miles, and that was where the road intersected with the road to Charlie Company. The Vietcong started harassing our mine sweeps with occasional sniper fire from the wooded areas. We would respond by calling in artillery on their position, and that was the end of the sniper fire.

Responding to sniper fire

Someone in supply contracted for a laundry in Trang Bang. It must be part of the culture because this place also came with girls. That was a benefit of belonging to recon platoon. We always got our laundry first.

We continued ambush patrols and set up ambush sites at night. A lot of men were getting injured by booby traps, and our platoon strength was very low. We had already lost six men when we lost Snyder, and that was just a week earlier. Our line companies took over some of the patrols while we trained replacements. One of our new replacements was Al, a first lieutenant who would become our platoon leader. Al seemed to be a pretty good guy; he was personable and professional and seemed to have a lot of common sense, something that seemed in short supply around here. I was now the most senior noncommissioned officer in the recon platoon, not counting the platoon sergeant, and Al wanted us to be close. So, it wasn't long until we became friends too. Al had worked as a sales rep for some large department store back In California. He thought I should do the same when my enlistment was up. But I wanted to be a career soldier.

It was time to get organized. Al wanted to send two jeeps to Charlie Company's location, where we could help them with their perimeter security, and it would provide us with the ability to sweep from that location to Trang Bang and meet with me when I arrived. It saved a lot of backtracking. The two jeeps I sent to Charlie Company were manned by SP/4 Anthony P., who also was from California, and SP/4 Jim W., who was from Nitro, West Virginia. Each of these men had a gunner and a driver for a total of six men; these people were equal in experience and ability.

Recon escort

Although I was having some issues with Jim W., some of the men were complaining that he was professing to be an atheist and that if God really existed, all this killing wouldn't be going on. The men were afraid that with all that talk he was a prime target for some of the mortars that we'd receive, and they didn't want to be around him when it happened. I decided to have a talk with Jim W. and advised him on what was being said. He agreed to tone it down but said he could believe what he wanted. Just a little more information on Jim W.: he was a fighter, and he always carried a sandbag with about half a dozen hand grenades just in case his rifle jammed, as had been the case with several of the newly issued M-16s. He had a real fear of getting pinned down without a functioning rifle and having Vietcong sappers, as we called them, getting their hands on him. These Vietcong sappers had a reputation of taking our dead and wounded and cutting off their privates and placing them in their mouths. This really bothered Jim, so he never went anywhere without an ample supply of hand grenades. If it hadn't been for his outspoken views on religion, I would have had him in my foxhole anytime.

I made the call and sent Jim W. and Anthony to Charlie Company. Things went well for a couple of days. We would sweep the roads, blow up booby traps, and meet Jim W. and Anthony at mama-san's laundry. Remember, *mama-san* was a generic name reserved for women of age and did not denote marital status. Jim W. was starting to enjoy his new role of leading. I noticed that he was having a strong influence on the men when I saw the supply of hand grenades in their jeeps. I had to smile.

July 10, 1967, started out just like any other day. We ate c-rations for breakfast and heated up some instant coffee by burning some of the C-4 plastic explosives and setting our canteen cups on the very hot little stove we had concocted from used c-ration cans. This one was a four burner. Not bad for a bunch of grunts. After breakfast, we mounted up and departed our base, sweeping the road as we went. I had positioned my jeep in the second position and was half watching the men sweeping and half scouring the wood lines for anything out of order. I had called Jim W. when we departed.

He said, "I'm on my way. See you in town."

"Roger out," I replied.

Just minutes later we heard over the radio, "Ambush down by the cemetery."

We could also hear the crackling of gunfire and a lot of yelling. Realizing the other men were under attack and they needed help, I decided to take a gamble on whether there were any mines or booby traps that might lie ahead in the road.

I gave the order, "Everybody mount up and follow me." I'd watched too many John Wayne movies not to have done it without a little flair. I told my driver, Dave B., to take the lead and head for the ambush site and to drive as fast as possible in hopes that if we hit a mine, we might get past it before it got us. We both knew better, but the gamble paid off. We arrived in Trang Bang within minutes and then turned to head for Charlie Company. We turned so fast that I thought for a moment we might roll the jeep. We didn't. My driver was doing exactly what I wanted. As we left the outskirts of Trang Bang, I could see our jeeps up ahead. They were smoldering, and there appeared to be a lot of chaos. I could see some

Vietcong still firing while they were trying to withdraw. I told my gunner to open fire on those to our right. He immediately started firing the .50-caliber machine gun, and I began firing my M-16 rifle as we continued to charge forward. The field to our right had a large growth of bamboo and a few large trees. I was concerned that more Vietcong might be hiding in the growth of bamboo. I could hear the jeep behind me starting to fire his m-60 machine gun. A multitude of thoughts were running through my mind, securing the area being foremost.

I called the tactical operations center. "Manchu six, this is Manchu Recon three. I need a dust off."

As my gunner continued to unload on the Vietcong, his spent cartridges started going down the back of my shirt, burning my neck, and sending a wave of nausea over me. I rearranged my position, raised my collar, and continued to fire. I told my driver to get as close to the lead jeep as possible, and he did. There was just enough room to walk between them. I told jeep three, with the 106-recoilless rifle, to hold back and set his sights on the bamboo thicket. The 106 had an anti-personnel round that could be set to explode at a distance determined by the gunner, and once it exploded, it would send out thousands of metal shards, destroying everything in its path—a very effective weapon. My driver and I disembarked, and I started assessing and reassessing our situation, while my gunner continued to lay down a field of fire. Everyone was yelling and screaming in pain as all of them had been wounded. Dave B. started yelling, "Jim is dead, Jim is dead!" I went to where Jim was lying next to his jeep and found him on his back, arms outstretched, his rifle in one hand and a grenade in the other. His ankles were crossed, and his head was slightly tilted and curiously pale white. Yes, he resembled Christ on the cross.

Now, before you think I've totally lost my mind, I should tell you that several of the men approached me and asked, "Did you see Jim W.? He looked like Christ on the cross."

"I know," was my reply.

We couldn't find a wound on Jim, and it wasn't until later that they discovered a small piece of shrapnel had entered right at the hairline on the back of his head and into his brain. Death had been instant, and there was not a mark on him. A couple of men just stood there and looked totally oblivious to what was going on around us.

Return fire started bouncing off my jeep, and I had to tell them to get down. I paused briefly to digest everything that was going on, everything I was seeing, but I had too much to do. I had to move on.

I started shouting orders. "Set up a perimeter; Dave B., tend to the wounded."

I called the sergeant on the 106 and instructed him to fire into the bamboo. I didn't know if anybody was hiding in there or not. "Take it out!" I ordered.

During all of this, Anthony P., the boy from California, was lying in a water-filled ditch about thirty yards away, screaming, "Mama, Mama," over and over and over.

I was back on the radio to the tactical operations center. "I need dust offs, two of them. I have one dead and four or five wounded."

In response I heard, "Use the phonetic alphabet."

I responded, "Get me some dust offs, dammit! I've got at least one kilo, India, alpha, and four or five whiskey, India, alpha."

Dave called me over to the driver of the first jeep. He was unsure of how to bandage the wounded man. The explosion that hit his jeep traveled up his legs, leaving his pants in shreds. The driver's scrotum was ripped open and his testicles, although still attached, were lying between his legs on the ground; they don't teach this in first aid. He had very little bleeding, so I told Dave to take a first aid packet and place the testicles against his groin and tie the ends to his belt both in front and back so they would stay in place. All the while, I was reassuring the driver that he would be okay. Return fire had ceased, so I told my gunner to cease-fire and then realized that the 106 never fired.

I called again and repeated the order, "Take it out."

The sergeant responded that he wanted to clear it with headquarters because he was concerned he might hurt some civilians. I told him it was a direct order. "If you can't do it, step down and turn command over to your gunner."

He fired, and that was the end of the bamboo. I'd deal with the sergeant later. He had committed a cardinal sin by disobeying a lawful order in combat. I couldn't let him slide if I wanted to, and I didn't want to. The troops had observed all of this, and you couldn't allow a breakdown in military order. They had to see there were consequences to not following orders. During all this, a brave medic rushed from Charlie Company on foot to help with the wounded. He gave Anthony a shot of morphine and placed a pressure bandage on his leg, where he had been shot in the thigh, he was still calling out, "Mama, Mama." I told him to give the driver that Dave was attending a shot of morphine. The gunner on jeep one came up and thanked me. He appeared to be in shock, and his abdomen was peppered with shrapnel. He kept saying how happy he was to see us coming to help and what a beautiful sight it was.

Over the radio I heard, "Dust offs arriving, throw smoke."

I popped a smoke grenade and threw it in the center of my perimeter. Anthony had quit screaming for his mother. He had bled out and died. I wondered if she heard him in her sleep. We placed our wounded on chopper one and our dead on chopper two and waved the pilots off, and as I did, the door gunner pointed out a group of civilians approaching with their hands up. There were about fifty of them, more than we were equipped to handle. I called headquarters and told them that we had cleared the area of our casualties. We now had about fifty civilians approaching with their hands up. We went ahead and herded the civilians to a spot alongside the road and had all of them sit with their hands over their heads. Headquarters called back and said that South Vietnamese police had been notified and they were sending transports for the civilians and they would handle the interrogations. Charlie Company would retrieve the jeeps and I could return to base as soon as the civilians were turned over. This gave me time to check out a hooch that was sitting nearby—too close not to know about the impending ambush. Dave B. and I went to the hooch and found an old woman and what I assumed was her mentally challenged son. He appeared to be in his early twenties. We ordered him to raise his hands and move away from the bed. He started mouthing us and giving us dirty looks and then started to come at us. In short, he didn't comply as quickly as he should have, so Dave hit him in the head with the butt of his rifle. I was proud of Dave for his quick response and the horizontal butt stroke.

Mama-san started screaming, and we shoved them out the door, forcing them to join the others. By this time the South Vietnamese police had arrived and were starting to load the civilians. I shook hands with the officer in charge and turned the mama-san and her son over to him. Things were calming down, and it was time for me to gather my troops and head for base camp. It was a quiet ride back to camp, everyone with his own thoughts. Our platoon sergeant met us at the gate and hopped into the back of my jeep. He wanted to know if I was okay.

"Sure, just a walk in the park," I said.

I saw the sergeant from the 106 slink away as we started to unload. I looked at the platoon sergeant and calmly said, "He'll never make it back if he goes out again." He was an old soldier and knew what I meant. But just in case he didn't, I went to the lieutenant and told him what happened.

Bob relaxing with some of the men in the squad. Second from right was wounded in July 10 ambush.

He said he'd been listening to the radio and he would take care of it. I don't know what transpired, but I never laid eyes on that sergeant again. I assume he was transferred to a line company. That was not a good thing for him. The gunner got a promotion and took charge of the 106. It had been a rough day, and I couldn't get Anthony's cries out of my head. A few days later, we got word from the South Vietnamese that we had killed two Vietcong and wounded several others in the exchange of fire.

Bob mourning our losses

July 10 was one of those days you never forget. I felt lot of mixed emotions: sadness over the loss of two men, pride in the way the men handled the situation, anger and disappointment in the sergeant on the 106. But today, I had proven my mettle. I had led a relief force into an ongoing firefight, suppressed the enemy fire, and saved several men.

Not a bad day's work for a twenty-year-old. Although we had lost two men, I couldn't help feeling proud of my behavior. You often wonder how you will react in a situation like that. I no longer had to wonder. Jim would have been damn proud. The next few weeks were almost uneventful except for the mortars we would receive at least a couple of nights a week. It was just enough to keep everyone on their toes.

Operation Rolling Thunder was an ongoing operation by the air force and navy where they would bomb suspected enemy supply routes, camps, and storage facilities with five hundred–pound and one thousand–pound bombs. At night, you could see the flashes of the exploding bombs from miles away. The ground would shake, as if there was an earthquake, and then you would hear the explosions. Hence, the name of the operation: Rolling Thunder.

CHAPTER 5

In August 1967, our battalion was being sent to sweep and assess bomb damage. This time we were leaving the jeeps behind and would be going on foot with the rest of the battalion. We would be picked up in the morning by the air cavalry and transported to a landing zone close to the Cambodian border. The landing zone was cold when we got there.

We formed up quickly and began our trek through jungle that was so thick you had a hard time seeing the sky. We were moving cautiously because of the likelihood of booby traps, and it wasn't long until somebody stepped on one. We secured the area and called for a dust off. It was the first time I ever saw them drop a line with a stretcher through the trees to pick up a wounded man. Usually they would be able to land, but the overhead canopy made landing an impossibility.

Eagle flight

We started moving again and started finding small bunkers and tunnels. The bunkers were empty, and the tunnels didn't reveal much more than a suspected underground hospital. We blew it up and continued to move. Finally, we started coming across the tremendous bomb strikes where there would be this large crater, and the surrounding trees and vegetation would be cleared for many yards all around. The craters were filled with clean blue water. Some of the guys wanted to go for a swim, but we didn't have the time. We were following the bomb run as we would encounter one crater after another.

It wasn't much farther when we started smelling the most disgusting and pungent odor you can imagine. It didn't take long to discover the source of the smell. The trees surrounding the craters were littered with body parts, along with burnt and shredded uniforms. They were everywhere but too many and too difficult to recover. We left them for the vultures. We did come across some graves, which the brass wanted dug up. They were desperate for a body count. The stench became so overpowering that some of the men were getting sick. We proceeded with our mission and turned in an estimate of the number killed. This had to be one of the most horrid sights a person would ever see. There were arms and legs, headless bodies, and bodiless heads everywhere you looked. It was truly like a walk through hell. We were getting close to the border, so we headed south with the sweep moving in three columns, headquarters being in the middle column with line companies on each flank. It was getting late, so we dug in for the night.

Morning came, and we continued sweeping, finding small bunkers, occasional booby traps, and several tunnels. We continued to blow everything up. We were in Charlie's backyard, but no Charlie. Once again, we dug in for the night.

The next morning, we moved to a clearing and were airlifted out and returned to base camp. August was slipping away, and I could mark another month off the calendar. I was getting anxious I guess. Monsoon season was setting in, and it was raining every day. We had ponchos to protect us from the increment weather, but it was steaming hot, and wearing the ponchos was like being in a sauna. You just couldn't win.

August 24 was my twenty-first birthday. The men gave me a tin of pound cake and a tin of peaches to go with it. The tins are about the size of a small tuna fish can for the cake and are about the size of a soup can for the peaches. Now, this was no small thing. Pound cake and peaches was one of the most favored by anyone who has had to live on C-rations and were always in demand. *Wow*! I was twenty-one; it was now legal for me to drink.

September came upon us, and I was at the halfway point of my tour. Sometime during the first week of September, Lieutenant Al, as I liked to call him, summoned me to his tent. He said, "I've got something for you," and handed me a pair of staff sergeant stripes. He said he thought I was too young to make E-6, so he waited until I turned twenty-one. I had not quite completed four years in the army, and I was only one pay grade below what my dad was when he retired. This was a proud, moment and I thanked him.

Newly promoted

The paperwork was usually slow catching up with us in the field, and I realized this when Al also handed me orders awarding me the combat infantryman's badge. This is an award that is coveted by everyone in the infantry and was dated May 1967.

We continued sweeping the roads and finally started getting some replacements. They were fresh from the States and green as grass. Just a bunch of FNGs.

Sweeping roads, flank security being deployed up front

My next assignment had me leading a road patrol with three jeeps and crews through several small villages. It was primarily to make an appearance and demonstrate our ability to control the area and keep the Vietcong guerillas out. It was a beautiful day when we started out, great temperatures and blue skies. We were approaching the first village when we realized something was wrong. The villagers were hiding in their huts, and no one was out working as they normally were. There were no kids or dogs out, just an eerie quiet. As we approached the center of the village, we could see a Vietcong flag flying from a tree right in front of the local mayor's hut. We set up in a defensive position while I started checking for booby traps. I was going to get that flag. I started up the tree while Dave B. kept warning me about booby traps. He wanted to get out of there. I did too, but not before I retrieved the flag. I took the flag and we left, not wanting to push our luck any further.

1967 captured Vietcong flag

The next day we were up at dawn and ready to hit the road. We were going to ride shotgun for an artillery unit that was moving out of our area. It was the morning of September 26, 1967. We got an early start and had received sniper fire before we had a chance to digest breakfast. Oh well, no one was hit, no harm, no foul. A helicopter gunship had silenced the sniper. We were getting close to where these guys were going to set up. They wanted us to move ahead and secure a stretch of road that they felt was particularly dangerous. We did. We stretched our platoon over a mile stretch of road and placed our jeeps facing away from the road in temporary positions. My jeep was facing a wood line about two hundred yards away, with rice paddies stretching between the road and the wood line. My gunner was manning the .50-caliber, and I was standing at the rear of the jeep, between it and the convoy of track vehicles that was starting to pass our position. They were moving past us when directly behind our jeep, one of the tracks hit an anti-tank mine. All I remember was the explosion and seeing the rear of the track vehicle rising into the air. The concussion hit me like a ton of bricks and threw me over the top of my jeep. I landed face first next to the rice paddy. I couldn't move but was somewhat aware that my gunner had landed on top of me. I'm not sure if that was intentional or not. He had grabbed the mike and started yelling, "Goff is dead, Goff is dead!" This wasn't the first time my gunner and I had disagreed on things, so as soon as I was able to regain my wits, I informed him that I wasn't dead.

Lieutenant Al came running up the road with map in hand to see how we were. He asked if I could walk, and I replied, "I think so, but get me out of here anyway."

He called for a dust off, giving them the coordinates, and it wasn't long until a chopper was there to pick me up. I had been knocked unconscious and had a piece of shrapnel in my left calf. The flight back to the hospital didn't take any more than fifteen minutes, enough time to come to my senses. They unloaded me onto a gurney and wheeled me into the entrance of the evacuation station. I was now sitting up to see what was going on around me. Several other casualties arrived just before me, and some were serious. The nurse said they would get to me as soon as they stabilized the others. My wound already had a pressure bandage on it, but the shrapnel was still there. I removed the shrapnel myself, as a part of it was sticking above the skin. The medical personnel cleaned up the wound and stitched me up. Once I felt that I was okay, I asked if I could return to my unit. They questioned me for a while and then agreed to send me back on light duty, with instructions to return and have the stitches removed. Somebody called my unit, and they sent a jeep to pick me up. I hobbled out on crutches and returned to my unit. I decided to call home when I got back. I wanted to be the one to tell them I had been wounded. It was the next day that I called home and spoke to Dad and Mom. I assured them I was okay. It was not bad enough to come home.

THE UNITED STATES OF AMERICA

TO ALL WHO SHALL SEE THESE PRESENTS, GREETING:

THIS IS TO CERTIFY THAT
THE PRESIDENT OF THE UNITED STATES OF AMERICA
HAS AWARDED THE

PURPLE HEART

ESTABLISHED BY GENERAL GEORGE WASHINGTON
AT NEWBURGH, NEW YORK, AUGUST 7, 1782
TO

STAFF SERGEANT E6 ROBERT L. GOFF, RA16774214, UNITED STATES ARMY

FOR WOUNDS RECEIVED
IN ACTION
26 SEPTEMBER 1967
REPUBLIC OF VIETNAM

GIVEN UNDER MY HAND IN THE CITY OF WASHINGTON
THIS   TWENTIETH   DAY OF   JUNE   1968

Stanley R. Resor
SECRETARY OF THE ARMY

F. K. FEARNS
Major General, USA
Commanding

Sue was working, and I wasn't sure which shift she was on. That's why my parents got the call. Dad agreed to call Sue and let her know that I was okay. Mom said she had been to a birthday party for a younger cousin of mine on the day that I was wounded. It really made me aware that it was a different world back home. I stayed at base camp the next week and must say I was starting to miss the action and wanted to return to my men. During my convalescence, we had a fragging incident. That's when some disgruntled soldier pitches a hand grenade into a superior officer's quarters. In this case it was the headquarters company commander. I don't remember if he lived or died. The military police sent the criminal investigators over to investigate. I do remember that they had one suspect, and they had him in custody.

Nui Bai Den in the distance to right

My stay at base camp had come to an end. The battalion along with recon was being sent to Nui Ba Den, a solitary mountain rising out of the plains. It looked out of place. The mountain was considered sacred to the Vietnamese, who believed it was a religious site and that Buddha had sat on this mountain at one time. Even though we weren't allowed on the mountain, special forces had set up a radio transmitting station on the very top, which could only be accessed by air. The corps of engineers operated a rock and gravel pit at the base of the mountain. The gravel was sorely needed for the dirt roads. So we had the top and the bottom, and Charlie had what was in between. The mountain was filled with tunnels, and that's where the bad guys were located. We weren't allowed to go after them or even to shell the mountain for fear of offending the South Vietnamese. The situation was very similar to what we have in Afghanistan now. Even when we know the enemy is in a mosque, you can't fire on it because it's supposedly sacred to the locals. More crazy rules of engagement. The mountain was known to be a staging area for the Vietcong to launch attacks from or to booby trap the roads. The engineers had the responsibility for clearing the roads, and that left us free to run med caps in the area. That's medical capabilities. We would escort medical personnel to the surrounding villages so they could immunize the children and tend to any medical needs anyone else had.

Bob making friends with the locals at the outskirts of their village

The Vietcong didn't like this because we were doing for the people something that they couldn't. It was a great propaganda tool for the United States and our allies.

I had asked Mom to send me a large box filled with penny suckers. She did, and we would pass them out to the kids whenever we got a chance. It turned out that med caps were a great opportunity to pass the suckers out. I don't think the kids had ever seen one, but that didn't stop them from asking for more. It was early October, and Dave B., my driver, was in Hawaii on R&R. That left me with the driving and my gunner on the .50 caliber. We had left our encampment and were patrolling the road around Nui Ba Den when I saw one of the engineer's dump trucks approaching from the other direction. The road wasn't wide enough to allow two vehicles to pass, so I decided I would pull as far over to my left as possible and allow the truck to pass on my right. The reason I pulled to the left was because it gave me the ability to lean out and check the berm for signs of a booby trap or mine, something I wouldn't be able to do if I had pulled to the right. As the truck approached, he began to slow down and pull over to his left. We waved to each other, and as he pulled even with us, there was an explosion that went off right under his gas tanks, which were located just behind the cab. The explosion blew the two engineers straight up and out of the truck. My gunner and I were blown out of our jeep and into a dried-up rice paddy that was next to us. The two engineers were shirtless, and fortunately the canvas top to the cab had been removed. Otherwise they might not have been blown out and their burns may have been worse. It was bad enough as it was, as the skin was peeling off their torsos, arms, and faces from the flames. My gunner and I were lucky again. We were shaken up quite a bit, as you might imagine, but nothing was seriously wrong.

Help was arriving from both directions and would aid the wounded. I remember looking at my gunner and tearing off my flak jacket.

I said, "I quit!"

I started to walk away from the scene when the battalion commander showed up. He asked, "Where are you going, Goff?"

I replied, "I quit," and I was serious.

He said, "What?" after laughing in disbelief.

So I repeated myself. "I quit!"

I went on to explain that the mines and booby traps were getting to me and how I had been blown over one jeep and out of another in just a matter of weeks. I was afraid my luck wouldn't last forever. I wanted off the jeeps.

The battalion commander was a soldier's soldier, and his next words were, "I understand. I can put you in S-2 intelligence. You'll be off the jeeps, but you'll still see action." I agreed, and that was the end of my assignment to recon.

Being in a recon platoon for just over seven months taught me how to survive. It teaches you to be hypervigilant, always on guard, always looking around, scanning the area, looking for anything or anyone out of place or anything that might present a danger. This isn't something that is taught as much as it is a habit you develop. It comes as a result of always looking for booby traps or potential ambush sites or watching to see if anyone poses a threat. You even had to be on guard against the kids as the Vietcong had been known to use them to drop a hand grenade in the back of your jeep as you were trying to help them. You were always watching the roads trying to find a spot where the dirt had been disturbed—afraid someone might have planted a mine. You learned and practiced these qualities to stay alive and to keep your buddies alive. Everyone learned or died. It was that simple. Learning these skills keeps you alive and makes you a better soldier. The only downside, and maybe it's not a downside, is that once you learn these skills or habits, you never forget them. You'll find that once you're back home, you continue to be hypervigilant—little things that most people are not aware of. I'll give you a couple of examples. One is sitting across from your wife or friend in a restaurant. He or she is talking to you, and you are listening or half listening while your eyes move from side to side to see what the movement was that you detected behind them. Just a customer leaving; no danger. You look the other direction to see if anything is out of the way. You do this not because you want to. It is now part of you; you have to do it. It's how you survived. It is how you *will* survive. As you go for a drive now, you look at the beautiful rolling hills, trees changing color, and birds flying south. It's a beautiful day. Those are the things most people would see. I see a good field of fire, a possible ambush site. I know it's not, because I'm home, but I still recognize the possibilities. Even when a flock of birds takes to flight, I think about what may have made them do so. Did they sense danger? These skill sets kept me alive. Now they keep me awake. It's called PTSD, post-traumatic stress disorder. Most combat veterans, at least the ones I know, are light sleepers. That's because a lot of the action was at night, and even when you were sleeping, you had to be ready to act. Mortars might start landing around you; you need to find cover quickly. The enemy attacks mostly at night; they like the cover of darkness to hide their movement, and once they start coming, you had *better* be ready.

So now you sleep lightly and dream about the ambushes and hear the faint cry of, "Mama, Mama" and wonder if there was anything you could have done differently. Unfortunately, some turn to drugs, some to liquor, just so they can sleep and not dream. Some suffer silently, and some just end it.

I reported to my new assignment at S-2 (intelligence). It was headed up by Capt. McDonald, and then there was me and SP/4 Carter. We had a Vietnamese interpreter assigned to our section, and our mission was to gather intelligence about the enemy, their movements, strengths, numbers, and any other information that might benefit our commanding officer. We received a couple of Chieu Hoi's (defectors from the Vietcong) who would be a part of the Kit Carson project. I would teach them a few English phrases and how to operate and maintain an M-16 rifle. They in turn would lead us to enemy bunkers, tunnels, and caches of food and supplies, which we would destroy. Sometimes, if possible, we would turn the food supplies over to needy civilians. Anytime we went out, we would place the Kit Carson Scouts in front. That way, if they led us into an ambush, they would be the first to die. This was understood by the scouts as well. We had several successful patrols that resulted in the destruction of large amounts of weapons and ammunition. On our last mission together, we received sniper fire, and while everyone was scurrying for cover, our scouts tripped a booby trap, resulting in multiple injuries to both. We pulled them back and requested a dust off. They quickly had a chopper on scene. After the dust off, we called for an artillery strike to silence the snipers and then returned to base.

The interpreter and I would accompany other patrols and gather whatever intelligence we could from enemy casualties. We would also take control of any prisoners and return to S-2 to interrogate them. One of the worst things about these patrols was the mosquitoes. There were more of them and they were larger than any I've ever seen. To this day, I can't stand mosquitoes. On one patrol, we ended up bringing two POWs in to be interrogated. Our interpreter became slick at getting information from these enemy soldiers. On this occasion, he blindfolded both men and put duct tape over the mouth of one. Both men were squatting, as they commonly, do when the interpreter started yelling questions at the one whose mouth was taped, saying, "Talk or die."

Bob with POWs

This went on for several minutes, and when there was no response, the interpreter pulled his .45 from the holster and fired one round into the air, kicking the man onto the ground. He then turned to the second prisoner and angrily asked him the questions the other one wouldn't answer. He told it all and couldn't tell it fast enough. Knowing that there are those who disagree with this, I will only say that these are the same Vietcong who would go into the villages at night, rape the village chief's wife, and mutilate his children by cutting their fingers or hands off because they had accepted medical help from the Americans or because the children were attending a South Vietnamese school.

We didn't take very many prisoners anyway; it seemed that they would rather fight to the death, and that was just fine with us. A lot of times before they would attack, they would get high on heroin or marijuana. That could have had something to do with them not giving up. Who knows?

We were well into November 1967, and the entire battalion was sweeping an area not far from the Cambodian border. I was traveling with the interpreter, Carter, and a few other guys from the headquarters section. It had been quiet, and we were about to settle down for a three-day truce for Thanksgiving. We would remain in the bush as a deterrent to the North Vietnamese and celebrate Thanksgiving by having our Thanksgiving meal flown out to us. We were told to dig in and prepare to stay in place for the three-day truce. As the battalion began digging in, I started looking for a spot for Carter, the interpreter, myself, and a few other guys from headquarters. I found a bamboo thicket that had a clearing in the middle large enough to accommodate maybe a dozen guys. There was only one path in, and that became a dead end. I think of it as a hillbilly cull de sac. It appeared to be a pretty good location for us to spend three days. There were six or seven of us who went in, laid our gear down, and began to dig in. As we were digging, one of the guys yelled, "Snake!"

Everyone looked in his direction and saw a very large cobra slithering our way, his head raised up and swaying back and forth as cobras do, in a very threatening manner. Here we were—some of America's finest, loaded to the teeth with rifles, pistols, hand grenades, machetes, and bayonets, and what did we do? We ran in as many directions as there were bodies. Nobody picked up a rifle or a machete! We just ran! Each of us made a new path through the bamboo. We thought we had the ideal location, but since there were so many ways in and out now, and knowing it was already occupied, we decided to go somewhere else.

Thanksgiving came, and we were served turkey and everything that went with it. The food was flown in by chopper in insulated mermac cans to keep it warm. I remember sitting on a fallen tree eating my Thanksgiving dinner and how it tasted as good as anything I could remember. The three days passed without incidence and we were on the move again.

The time had come for me to go on R&R, and I chose to spend my five days in Hawaii. Coming home wasn't an option. We only had five days and the military was concerned that some would not return. Sue was going to meet me at the Ilikai Hotel. We had a room overlooking the beach. She arrived first, and I flew in a few hours later. She had been sick on the flight over and wasn't quite over it. She was fighting it, not wanting to waste a moment together, but didn't shake it until the next day. We enjoyed the night life and took in the club scene. I was starting to drink every night, but we blew it off to the party scene, not realizing that it ran a lot deeper. This became a form of self-medication. We did get to go swimming though, and enjoyed our time together. She was a real trooper and did what she could to make the most of our time together. We visited some of the sites but always ended up back at the Ilikai Club enjoying the band and drinks, of course. There was no adjusting. Vietnam was always with me, always on my mind. The five days passed quickly, and it wasn't long until I was on my way back to Vietnam. Sue and I said our good-byes as she held back the tears, and I thought about the possibility of making it home after all. It all seemed surreal.

In December 1967, I was back, and it felt like I never left. I spotted one of the guys from recon approaching, along with another soldier. "Somebody wants to see you, Sarge."

I recognized the young trooper now. He was the driver on jeep one at the ambush back on July 10. I said, "Good to see you soldier; I almost didn't recognize you with your pants on."

We all laughed. He said he wanted to thank me before he headed back to the rear; obviously he had been reassigned to the rear. He was only nineteen and just got married before coming to Vietnam. All of us wondered how he was. We hardly ever heard anything about someone who was evacuated. He said at first, they told him he would never have children and might not be able to have relations. But as it turned out, they were wrong on both counts. Now that's a real infantryman.

He was beaming as he told us all the details and expressed his gratitude for us coming to their aid. We were happy for him, and it was not often that you had a happy ending there. Because he had to leave, he wanted to make sure he got to see me first. He awkwardly leaned over, gave me a quick hug, and said, "Take care, Sarge."

I hugged him back and replied, "You too."

Working in S-2 intelligence allowed me some insight into what we were up against. From all the chatter and reports of enemy activity, one could only conclude that the North Vietnamese were building up for an offensive. We had reports of increased activity along the Cambodian/Vietnamese border, and our battalion was sent to patrol the border area and intercept units of the North Vietnamese Army. We were participating in an operation named Yellowstone. We were given instructions not to enter Cambodia or fire into it; more politically correct rules of engagement. It was December 11, and we had been sweeping all day. We dug in that evening, and around midnight the enemy started mortaring our position. It was the most precise shelling I have ever witnessed. They walked those shells across our position with uncanny precision time and time again. The NVA were so close we could see the flashes as the mortars were leaving their tube. It seemed like it would never end, and rounds were dropping all around us. When the shelling started, our battalion executive officer started yelling not to fire back because they were in Cambodia. The shells were landing so close to our foxholes that the explosion was causing some of the dirt around the top of our hole to start caving in. We were scared and stayed as low in the foxhole as we could. There was nothing else that we could do. It's times like this when you start praying, and that night was no exception. During a lull in the shelling, the sergeant major started yelling for me. I didn't want to come out of my foxhole at first, so I considered not answering.

He yelled again, "Goff, we need you!"

So I got out of my hole and ran to his position. When I got there, I saw that they had a wounded man lying on the ground with a medic hovering over him, working to seal a sucking chest wound and stop some of the bleeding. A sucking chest wound is when the lung or lungs have been pierced and you need to stop the air from going into the lung from the entry wound. This can be done by placing nonporous material, such as plastic, over the entry wound and placing a first aid packet over the plastic and compressing it tightly enough so air can't enter the lung. Hopefully, this will keep the lung from collapsing and allow for time to transport the individual to a hospital. Once the medic finished with him, four of us would carry him to a dust off that was due to arrive any minute.

We could hear the chopper coming, and suddenly he lit up the landing zone with a spotlight. I remember thinking this had to be the stupidest helicopter pilot in the entire army. We were still engaged with the enemy, and this dummy was lighting us up. We used a poncho as a litter, and four of us half carried and half dragged this poor guy to the chopper. The poncho was slick with his blood and gritty with the sand that was all around. This almost made it impossible to hold on to. My hands kept slipping; it felt like sandpaper cutting your fingers, and all I could think about was the North Vietnamese sighting in on the chopper and all of us getting blown to hell.

We got him loaded, and as the chopper started to leave, we could hear the *whoomph, whoomph, whoomph* of mortars being fired. We got back to our holes as quickly as we could. The mortars started landing.

Once again, the battalion executive officer started yelling, "Hold your fire! They're in Cambodia."

Finally, one of the guys from Alpha Company decided this was enough and yelled back, "expletive deleted you, **expletive deleted**." Then he opened fire with an m-60 machine gun and everyone else joined the party. It only took a few minutes for the mortars to become silent. Nobody mentioned the fact that we had fired into Cambodia or that we had been instructed not to. Due to the accuracy of the mortar attack, we lost a couple of Manchus that night.

An intel report from division said we had been hit by a combination of North Vietnamese regulars and Vietcong guerillas who were trying to infiltrate into South Vietnam. They were going to attempt to go around us. History now shows that this was part of the buildup for the famous Tet Offensive by the North Vietnamese that would occur in the coming weeks. Tet is the Vietnamese new year and is celebrated on January 31.

During the next few days after December 11, we continued to sweep the area. As we advanced, the headquarters company was supposed to be flanked by two line companies and they would provide our flank security. Shortly after moving out, we started receiving sniper fire from our right flank. It was obvious that our flank security wasn't there. It's a good example of how easy it is to become disoriented in the jungle. We hit the ground as the bullets were cracking right over our heads. It didn't seem like I could get low enough. There was a medium-sized tree directly behind me that I wanted to get behind, but as I looked around, I could see where bullets had struck the tree about twelve to fourteen inches off the ground. It wasn't safe for me to move. I heard someone give the order to throw smoke. Smoke would keep the sniper from being able to see us—a great idea. Seconds later, I heard the pop of a smoke grenade. Unfortunately, no one had checked to see which way the wind was blowing. As the smoke started drifting back over our position, you could hear some of the men coughing. The battalion commander hurried past my position, heading to the rear and giving the order to pull back. I followed him as quickly as I could, and we held up after we put about two hundred yards between us and the sniper. Some of the men who followed us started drawing machine gun fire. Fortunately, nobody was wounded. The colonel was laughing about the smoke as he called in for an air strike. We sat there and only had to wait about five minutes before the lead pilot asked us to throw smoke so he could identify our position. We threw smoke, which he identified as yellow, and was confirmed by the colonel. The colonel followed up by saying the machine gun was approximately 250 meters to our front. Within seconds the first jet flew by our position so low that we could see the pilot. He went in with guns blazing, and as he pulled up, we could hear him telling the other pilot that the target was a .50-caliber machine gun. A .50 caliber could down a jet if he hit it. The second jet came in much the same as the first, only this time he was firing rockets, and as he pulled up he said to the first pilot, "Target eliminated!" After some small talk with the pilots, the colonel gave the order to continue the sweep. Only this time they made sure the line companies were on our flanks. We continued our sweep without any further resistance.

It was December 18. We were getting ready to move out. Word was received that we would be picked up and flown to Bo Tuc. An old French fort used to be there but was destroyed by the Vietnamese back in the mid-'50s. Scuttlebutt was that the North Vietnamese were trying to skirt around us. We were being sent to block them. Our entire battalion would have to go along with a battery of 105 artillery. I was on the last eagle flight to arrive along with Alpha Company. An eagle flight is where you have many helicopters transporting troops to or from a specific location.

When the first units arrived, they immediately started receiving sniper fire and an occasional mortar round or two—a hot landing zone. This caused them to have to dig in quickly and resulted in our perimeter being too small for all four line companies. This caused a lot of confusion and caused them to set up another line inside the perimeter. This was part of Alpha Company, and they were told to dig two-man holes between the outside perimeter and the battery of 105s. I was told to dig in close to the tactical operations center. The ground was soft, so it didn't take long for a kid named Toby and me to dig in. Toby worked for the old man and was a real nice kid. I don't know why I call him a kid. The average age over here is only nineteen or twenty, and I had just turned twenty-one. I guess it was having to be responsible for so many that made me feel older. We didn't have the material to construct a top for our foxhole, so we had to leave it open. We were continuing to receive sniper fire and occasional mortars for the remainder of the day. I didn't have a good feeling about this; our battalion strength was down. There were probably no more than six hundred in the field, if that. Intel reports were talking about two NVA regiments and possibly a battalion of Vietcong. A regiment consists of four battalions. If the reports were true, that meant we could be outnumbered by eight or ten to one. Those odds are great at a dance hall, but out there it only meant one thing: trouble, big trouble! I normally only carried 140 to 160 rounds of ammo for my M16. That day I was carrying twice that and about half a dozen grenades. I learned something from Wears as well. There were several old open wells within our perimeter, so you had to be careful not to walk into one of them since they weren't marked. Everything considered, we settled down in our foxhole and waited for the inevitable attack that everyone knew was coming. We took turns trying to sleep but were unable to get much rest. The adrenaline was running on high. At about 3:00 a.m. we started receiving mortars. We got down as low as we could and hoped that one of the mortars wouldn't land in our foxhole. Our foxhole was located close to the front of the tactical operation center. We were their last line of defense, and they were our Alamo. I didn't like to think like that, but that's the way it was that night. Suddenly there was a lull in the mortars, and our perimeter started firing like crazy. We knew that this was nothing like we had ever seen before, but there wasn't anything we could do except wait. It was dark, and all you could see were the flashes coming from the individual weapons. The next thing we knew was that the artillery battery's stockpile of ammunition was exploding and going everywhere. We had been overrun, and they had blown the artillery's ammunition up. The shells of our own ammunition were landing all around us. You wanted to run, but there was no place to go. It reminded me of a fireworks display that went horribly wrong. There was a whole lot of confusion, with people shouting and yelling and running about as our line began to crumble. The colonel gave the order for everyone to stay in their holes and shoot to kill anything that moved, the NVA were inside the perimeter. My heart was beating out of my chest as we heard people running but still could only see by the flashes of gunfire. Suddenly there was a figure to my front moving to my right and moving fast. I couldn't get turned fast enough to get off a shot. I knew there would be more and warned Toby to keep looking one way while I looked the other; I just missed one off to my right. We tried to keep each other informed on what we were seeing. Somebody finally started lighting up some parachute flares. This helped at first, but then it seemed that everybody who was out of a hole would hit the dirt as soon as the flares lit up.

The flares were great as long as they lasted but ruined your night vision when they burned out.

I yelled, "Toby, he's coming," and as he started to turn, I fired a quick burst.

Bodies of enemy KIA

Bodies of enemy KIA

The flare burned out; I didn't even know if I hit him or if he just went down. Toby was turned around my way by now trying to see what I was shooting. More flares went off. I could see where he went down, but I wasn't sure if he was hit or playing possum, so I aimed at his head and fired a single shot. He was dead. I remember feeling a great sense of relief—nothing else. Better him than me.

The ammo dump continued to explode, and shells continued to land everywhere. It seemed like the whole place was on fire, at least we could see. The 105s started firing beehive rounds point blank at the enemy. A beehive is an anti-personnel round that can be fired directly at the enemy. They must not have blown all the ammo. Thank God.

Jets were starting to come in now and were strafing the enemy. "Just keep them off our asses, boys!"

Enemy KIA

As dawn started to approach, the intensity of the fighting was beginning to ease up. "Thank you, Lord, and thank you to the pilots who always go above and beyond to pull us ground troops out of the crap."

The next morning, we found that we had ten men killed and thirty-five wounded. We constantly had helicopters flying in and out, taking out the wounded, and then the dead, and returning with ammo. While searching the inside of the perimeter, we found where an NVA soldier had fallen into one of the open wells. We had the interpreter try to talk him out, but he wasn't having any of it. Tired of trying, one of the guys dropped a grenade down the well. Add one to the body count. It took a while to gather the NVA bodies, of which there were about fifty. We had to gather their weapons and check them for matters of intelligence (maps, letters etc.). I went over to the guy who was coming at me last night, as much out of curiosity as anything. I started to search his belongings for matters of intelligence. There wasn't much, but I did find a picture in his wallet. It had been carefully wrapped in plastic to protect it from the elements. It was obvious to me that the picture was special to him.

Enemy KIA

As I began to unwrap it, I could see it more clearly, and I realized its significance. It was a picture of him and a very attractive Vietnamese woman cradling a baby in her arms. They were standing in front of a war memorial; both were smiling. I looked over at him and realized for the first time how young he was. He couldn't have been any more than my age. I folded the plastic back around the picture and placed it in his shirt pocket so he could be buried with it. In the beginning, my mind would often wander back and wonder what ever happened to the wife and the baby. It was almost Christmas, and my thoughts kept returning to a little orphan in Hanoi. Merry Christmas, son. Merry Christmas.

CHAPTER 6

We hadn't taken any prisoners from the night's battle, and as dawn appeared, it was obvious they had taken their wounded with them. We found a lot of blood trails leading away from Bo Tuc. I don't have a clue as to how Toby and I got out of that alive. Some of the men got involved in hand-to-hand combat. Toby and I were lucky. Nobody got that close. After cleaning up, they decided it was time for a break and airlifted us back to base camp. I was never so glad to hear that *thump, thump, thump* of the Hueys as they descended from the sky to take us back to base camp. This gave us an opportunity to shower and get some hot food and some much-needed rest. Christmas was here, and we were receiving a lot of packages from home. I couldn't help but think of that little boy in the picture. I went over to visit with recon and saw some of the men whose faces would be with me forever. We got a lot of homemade cookies and other baked goods for Christmas that we all shared. Dave B's mother won the award for the best chocolate chip cookies. I liked them so much that Dave had his mom send them to me for Christmas for several years after I was discharged; God love her. I remember getting a huge box of Hickory Farms from my Uncle John and Aunt Rose.

Christmas and New Year's passed, but not before we were treated to a USO show. It seems that we were going to have some Puerto Rican girls/dancers perform for us. Not exactly Bob Hope and Raquel Welch, but we were a little farther out than where they normally went. They were pretty good, but what the hell, we'd take anything at this point. Everyone enjoyed the show, and there was plenty of beer to go around. The dance troupe was going to spend the night, so they were billeted in the mess tent with military police guarding the doors. You know, the temptation was too great, and some of the guys convinced me that since I had been in recon, I should find a way in. Well, it had been a long year, and I'd had enough beer that I thought, *Why not?* We got as close to the mess tent as we could without being seen. It was time to go into my stealth mode. I began to low crawl across this open space, heading for the middle of the tent, thinking, *If I can get there, all I'd have to do is lift the side of the tent and slip in.* Well I made it, lifted the side, and there was enough room to slide under. I couldn't wait to get back and tell the others. So, I started crawling back and made it undetected, but the guys weren't there. I got up and hunched over, started running back to our quarters to tell them the good news. Just as I was approaching the hooch, my left foot couldn't find the ground. I had just stepped into a six-foot-deep trench that was being constructed as a shelter for mortar and rocket attacks, my right knee bent sideways, and if I hadn't been drunk I'm sure it would have killed me. That's how bad it hurt. I let out a yell, and the guys came running. After they stopped laughing, they pulled me out and took me to the dispensary. It wasn't easy explaining what was going on at that time of night, but I guess they felt sorry for me, because they went ahead and bandaged my knee, put me on crutches, and told the guys to let me sleep it off. I had a severe strain, but nothing was broken except for my pride. The guys were still laughing as they half carried me back. They all wanted to know what had happened, so I told them, "I was trying to find you guys so I could tell you that I found a way in." You could have heard a pin drop.

Base camp under mortar attack; petroleum tanks hit

"Well, you have to show us."

"I can't. I'm on bed rest."

I had the last laugh. I was a short timer now, and I was spending a lot more time at base camp, hobbling around on crutches. I was starting to get a little bored, but not enough to volunteer for anything outside the wire. Hell, I wasn't even going on laundry runs if I didn't have to. One of the guys from recon brought my laundry to me. He said he was going that way anyway.

It was January 30–31, and the Vietnamese were celebrating Tet, the Vietnamese new year. The Vietcong units were surging into action over the length and breadth of South Vietnam. In more than a hundred cities and towns, shock attacks by Vietcong sappers/commandos were followed by wave after wave of supporting troops. By the end of the city battles, thirty-seven thousand Vietcong troops deployed for Tet had been killed. Many more had been captured or wounded, and the fighting had created more than a half-million civilian refugees. Casualties included most of the Vietcong's best fighters, political officers, and secret organizers. For the guerrillas, Tet was nothing less than a catastrophe. On February 23, over thirteen hundred artillery rounds hit the Marine base at Khe Sanh, more than on any previous day of attacks. Our battalion had been sent to sweep the areas surrounding Saigon. Saigon and Tan Son Knut had been receiving numerous rocket attacks.

Intelligence had said that elements of a North Vietnamese regiment were in the area, and they were responsible for the rocket attacks. The battalion had been sweeping the area since February 25; initially the battalion was suffering at least two casualties every day. On March 1 Bravo Company was again pinned down by a significant communist force. Several were killed or wounded, and they were eventually forced to withdraw with the assistance of Alpha Company. Because of this action, the plan for March 2 was for airstrikes and artillery to strike into this same area, followed by an assault by companies A, C, and D, with Company B in reserve. Charlie Company would lead the way, followed by Companies D and A. At 9:00 a.m. on that fateful day, Charlie Company came under heavy fire from a large enemy force concealed in bunkers and spider holes. The initial barrage lasted approximately eight minutes, but sniper fire by rear guard elements hindered movement by Companies D, A, and B for much of the day. Charlie Company lost forty-nine men on that day, along with twenty-four wounded. That was the worst single-day loss our battalion had suffered during my twelve months in Vietnam. Although I was on a cane, I felt obligated to fly to Tan son Knut to help identify the dead. It turned out to be a gruesome sight: body bags and blood everywhere.

THE UNITED STATES OF AMERICA

TO ALL WHO SHALL SEE THESE PRESENTS, GREETING:
THIS IS TO CERTIFY THAT
THE PRESIDENT OF THE UNITED STATES OF AMERICA
AUTHORIZED BY EXECUTIVE ORDER, 24 AUGUST 1962
HAS AWARDED

THE BRONZE STAR MEDAL

TO

STAFF SERGEANT E-6 ROBERT L. GOFF, RA16776244, UNITED STATES ARMY

FOR
MERITORIOUS ACHIEVEMENT
IN GROUND OPERATIONS AGAINST HOSTILE FORCES

IN THE REPUBLIC OF VIETNAM FROM APRIL 1967 TO APRIL 1968

GIVEN UNDER MY HAND IN THE CITY OF WASHINGTON
THIS   SIXTH   DAY OF   MARCH   1968

F. K. MEARNS
Major General, USA
Commanding

SECRETARY OF THE ARMY

I only had four days left in country. It was hard to believe that I'd made it that far. It had only been a year, but it seemed like a lifetime; for some it was. I went down to recon's position to say my good-byes and see the men I felt so incredibly close to. I thought it would be a happy day, but truth was, I felt a little sad at having to leave those guys, with whom I had been through so much. We truly were a band of brothers, and I knew I would miss them. At least I left them with some good stories.

I had two days left. I was supposed to hitch a ride to Tan Son Knut on a CIA plane in the morning with another guy from my unit who was also rotating back. His name was Tom Jorden; he was a specialist E-4. The day had arrived; Tom and I were at the airstrip waiting for the CIA guys to show up. They were running a little late, but they finally made it. It was only about a thirty-minute flight to Tan Son Knut, so we had plenty of time on our hands before we got on the "freedom bird"—at least thirty-six hours. We were supposed to process out and spend the night on the other side of the base. We went ahead and processed out, but skipped the billeting assignments. We were going to downtown Saigon to spend the night and have a little fun. We found a nice restaurant in Saigon and settled down to eat the first steak dinner that we had had in a long time. It wasn't bad at all for water buffalo. I think we would've eaten anything that didn't come in a can, to tell the truth. We proceeded to a nightclub that catered to American GIs. We had some good laughs as we listened to a Vietnamese singer do his imitation of Elvis Presley. After a few drinks, we went to the hotel, had a shower with real hot water, and slept in a real bed. Boy, it felt good!

The next morning, we grabbed a taxi and had him drive us to the airport. They had military police at the gate, and when we got out of the taxi, they just sort of looked at each other in disbelief. We showed them our orders to go to the States, and they just smiled and waved us through. No GIs were allowed downtown unless they were on official duty or had a pass. We went directly to the terminal and signed in. Our flight would be leaving in one hour. Both of us were getting a little anxious. I know I wasn't expecting to get this far—not on foot anyway. The hour passed quickly, and we were starting to board the freedom bird, as it was commonly known. After going to our assigned seats, I began to look around and started recognizing faces—faces that I remembered from the flight I took to get to Vietnam. For now, we mostly nodded in recognition and smiled. Everyone on the plane was unusually quiet, except for the stewardesses, who were all smiles and welcoming us aboard. They started closing the doors, and I think everyone on board was holding his breath. Nothing had been said by anyone other than the flight personnel. We started to taxi. I looked around, and still no one said a word. I could see some white knuckles on the armrests. The plane turned around at the end of the runway, and the pilot started to crank up the engines. There was still no conversation. We started to proceed down the runway, and I think everyone was waiting for the plane to take a hit. Still nothing. The nose of the plane started to lift up, and as the plane picked up speed, the wheels soon followed. Still nothing. We were gaining altitude, and then we started to level off. Still nothing. In just a couple of minutes, we started to go over the ocean, and as we did, there erupted a roar and the clapping of hands like you would not have believed. Nobody was going to say anything until we were out of range. It was just unbelievable. We had a long flight ahead of us, and we would be stopping in Japan to refuel. We would be allowed off the plane during this process, but we weren't allowed to leave the terminal. I don't think any of us wanted to get out of sight of that plane. Once airborne, we could leave our seats, and for those of us who recognized some of the other passengers, it was like a high school reunion.

"I remember you from the flight over," was said by several.

You could see tears running down the cheeks of some, and a couple were sobbing; most couldn't believe we'd made it. Thoughts of home started running through my mind, and I wondered how everyone would react. I knew I'd changed, but would they see it? It was kind of funny that we were leaving a country where it was okay to just shoot people and you didn't think twice about it, and now I was worried if anyone was going to notice the change in me. We all wanted to be accepted, and I guess that was my concern. We had read and been told of all the turmoil with the war protesters and didn't know what to really expect when we got home.

It was a long flight, but we were finally approaching California. When we landed at Oakland, the buses pulled up to the plane so we could begin our ride to the military installation. It was obvious to some that they didn't want us deplaning and walking through the civilian terminal. That was okay with me as I was still using a cane to get around with. When we got off the buses, they quickly started processing us. They didn't want to delay us any more than they had to. I got a new uniform and had to throw away the old. We took showers and shaved, and while we did that, our uniforms were being prepared. They had to sew everyone's rank on, along with the division patch with which you served. We were issued new shoes, socks, and underwear. The paymaster gave us the money that we were due, along with airline tickets to our destination. We were fed a nice steak dinner, and they said they would transport us to the airport as soon as we finished eating.

The next announcement was, "If anyone needs the services of a chaplain or a psychiatrist, form up on the left. Everyone else to the right to go to the airport." Everyone went to the right. Imagine that!

We boarded the buses and took a short trip to the airport. As we unloaded, I noticed a flight of stairs that we would have to go up. At the top, there were a handful of war protestors. Several police officers went up and moved them to the side. There were three busloads of troops unloading to board flights home.

On the way up the stairs, one of the soldiers said to the officers, "If you need help, just holler."

The officers just smiled, and the protesters didn't say a word. They didn't need to. The sign said it all: "Baby Killer."

CHAPTER 7

My next assignment was as an instructor at the Recondo School at Fort Carson, Colorado. I was teaching patrolling, navigation, map reading, rappelling, escape, and evasion. We learned a lot in Vietnam, and we were passing that knowledge and experience on to these guys, in hopes that this knowledge would keep them alive when the time came for them to fight. I felt at home leading these men through the mountains of Colorado. It was like I was back with recon. It felt good. But if I was going to change my MOS, I needed to get on with it. MOS stands for military occupational skill. I wanted to change my MOS to military police so I could work my way into criminal investigations. This would be a career move that would give me room to advance and a skill set that I could take anywhere. I transferred over to the 548th military police battalion and began learning all I could about police work and spent some time as a guard commander at the local stockade. Within six months, I had a secondary MOS of 95 B, that's military police. I was in the process of getting it changed to be my primary MOS when I was put on notice that I was going to have to return to Vietnam as an infantry sergeant.

I decided not to go.

I was hoping I'd left all those feelings and emotions behind me when I left Vietnam, only to have them slap me in the face. I went to personnel and tried to get the orders changed to military police. They denied my request and said they needed infantrymen more than they needed police. Well, no kidding. I didn't have enough time left on my enlistment to complete a tour in Vietnam, so I decided I would get out if they weren't going to let me go as a military policeman. They said they still needed infantry, so I decided not to reenlist. I had seen enough. I received my honorable discharge on July 1, 1970, and relocated my family to West Virginia, where most of my family now resides.

Aware that I had an exemplary military record, I thought it would be easy to find a job and settle down. It didn't take long to realize that there was a lot of resentment about the war and very few people were hiring veterans. I was unemployed for nine months before I got a job with the West Virginia Department of Labor—a job that would last for thirty years. I was having nightmares and drinking to try and forget. They say that the constant action day after day had created a high level of adrenaline, which we became addicted to, and that's why we drank and sought action. Vietnam vets have a high percentage of divorces, and I was no exception. The medical field didn't come up with a diagnosis until the late seventies— too late for some of our fighting men. Adjusting wasn't always easy, but I made it, quit drinking and was able to transition my military job skills to civilian life.

I entered my employment as a trainee and worked my way up to the position of Director of the Wage and Hour section for the state of West Virginia, from which I retired in 2001. That was the year I decided to run for city council, and I was sworn in on January 2, 2002. It was an interesting adventure, although I continued to be haunted in my dreams—dreams of ambushes and the cries of the wounded. These memories would never go away. We just had to move on—move on and deal with it.

Serving on city council enabled me to help others and to give back to the community that had supported me. It also had its challenges; politics always does.

I served with some fine people on council and someone I considered a friend was the mayor. We had differences of opinion on some issues that were complicated by my PTSD. Whenever I felt like I was being attacked, I would follow the training I'd received in the army and counterattack—ride to the sound of the guns, as they would say. Sounds familiar, doesn't it? Ever since Vietnam, I've never turned away from adversity. Maybe I should. I could go on about PTSD and how it raises its ugly head when you least expect it, but I'd have to write a book. Not all traits of PTSD are bad. Hypervigilance is one trait that I wouldn't give up even if I could. You are always on guard and aware of your surroundings. It's seldom that you're surprised. When I take the time to reflect on those years on council, I realize we accomplished a lot of good, despite our differences.

During that period, I paid a visit to the Vietnam memorial wall along with my wife, Sarah, and left a message on the virtual wall {internet} to my good friend Jim Snyder. The message was just recently discovered by Jim's niece, and she attempted to contact me in search of information about Jim. I inadvertently lost her contact information and had to ask my wife for help in trying to locate this family. Sarah's much better on the computer than me. She was successful in locating Jim's sister, Cindy. I was concerned by what Cindy's reaction might be when she discovered that her brother died when he volunteered to replace me on a patrol. However, I felt that I should talk to them and that possibly I could give them some comfort since Jim and I were so close. I sent Cindy a message on Facebook identifying myself and asking her if she was in fact Jim's sister. She responded immediately. She said yes and that she wanted to know everything I could tell her about her brother.

We messaged each other for hours, and she finally asked, "Do you know whose place Jim took on patrol the day he died?"

My heart was in my throat when I said, "Cindy, I was that soldier."

I didn't know what to expect, but it certainly wasn't what she said next. She said, "I knew it, I just knew it," and then went on to say what a burden I must have carried all that time and that she didn't want me to carry it any longer. She said, "Jim would do it all over again. I know he would, and he wouldn't want you to carry that burden." We talked a lot that day and ever since. She wanted to meet me and I really wanted to meet her. She was only eighteen when he died and she had a lot of unanswered questions; specifically, did he suffer? I knew that he hadn't and assured her of that. She seemed to be relieved, and for that I am grateful. We agreed to meet at the Vietnam memorial on June 27, the fiftieth anniversary of his death. I believed this would be a time of healing for Cindy as well as me. This will be full circle for me, and I thank God for the opportunity.

Sarah and I would be leaving for the wall to meet Jim's sister in one week. I was really looking forward to it. June 26 came along, and it was time to pack and head for the wall in Washington, DC. It was a beautiful day for the trip, blue skies and lots of sunshine. My wife, Sarah, was just as excited as I was to meet Cindy and her family. She had heard the stories about

Vietnam and Sgt. Jim Snyder. She had shared my nightmares for thirty years, and I couldn't have had a better partner or wife. We wondered what it would be like to finally meet this family, and I wondered if I would ever find any peace from the guilt I felt about Jim's death. We spent the night in Washington, DC, at the Trump Hotel. We decided to splurge since this was a special occasion, and we went on to prepare to meet the family in front of the wall where Jim's name is engraved. We were going to meet the next morning at 10:00. Sarah and I arrived early, along with Jill, a lifelong friend of Sarah's who wanted to come along and add her support.

Well, ten o'clock came and went, and no Cindy. We found a bench in the shade and watched all the people walking along the wall, stopping at a name, a brother, a father, a grandfather, all paying their respects to men lost in war fifty years ago. Fifty some thousand names in all. It's a visit that tugs at your heart, even if you don't know any of those whose names appear on the wall. Cindy called. They were lost in DC traffic, and if that wasn't enough, their daughter Brandi was sick and her husband had taken her to the hospital. Cindy made sure Brandi was going to be okay before proceeding to the wall. Their day wasn't getting off to a very good start, but they found their way, and we were about to meet for the very first time. We spotted them about fifty feet away appearing hot and hurried. Cindi and I embraced, and I think we both sighed a sigh of relief. For me it was the culmination of a fifty-year journey—fifty years to the day since my friend, Cindy's brother, had died. Cindy and I stood in front of Jim's name in the middle of that long, long black wall, arms around each other, silently comforting one another's wounds from long ago. Standing there with Cindy, in front of that wall with Jim's name etched into the granite, I couldn't help but think back to that fateful time and remember the last few hours that Jim and I had together. We had some downtime the night before and shared C- rations for dinner, talking about home and how nice it would be to see our families and friends. The men in our platoon were cleaning their weapons and getting ready for the next day. Jim was a short timer and scheduled to return to the States in just a couple of weeks. I remember telling him he shouldn't be going out, but he insisted, saying it would be routine and he would be back before you knew it. The next morning, we had a hot breakfast thanks to the mobile mess. We had the army's favorite: powdered eggs and hamburger gravy on toast. It was a normal day. Jim started getting his patrol together as we parted and said our, "See ya later," but we didn't … After my call, I quickly learned that our patrol had been hit. My heart skipped a beat as I started thinking about who it could be and all the possibilities. My worst nightmare was about to arrive. The first chopper landed with the wounded, and one of the men told me it was a Chinese claymore mine and that Jim and the lieutenant were KIA. Words will never express the feelings

I had when I learned that Jim had died on a patrol that I should have been on. He was my buddy and best friend. I knew I was going to miss this guy in my life.

Standing at the wall with Jim's sister and thinking how all of this came to pass reminded me of the pain I've carried all these years.

Cindy and Bob, June 27, 2017

As if reading my mind, she suddenly turned to me and in hushed tones said, "I can't believe you've carried this for all these years." Once again she said, "I don't want you to carry it any longer. Jim wouldn't want it either. I know Jim, and I know he would do it all over again."

I couldn't help but think how much this gracious lady was just like her brother. We continued to stand there, her asking questions about his last days and what his life was like in Vietnam. I answered them one by one, realizing that she'd had these questions all this time. Cindy is as much of a casualty of war as any of us who had to fight it.

Cindy and Bob June 27, 2017

We decided we would go to lunch and get out of the hot sun. Lunch was at a restaurant just a few blocks from the hospital where Brandi and her husband were dealing with the emergency. I can only imagine what that was like. She was the one responsible for Cindy and me getting together, and she didn't even get to participate. She wouldn't have been able to get a word in, as Cindy, her husband, Billy, Sarah, and I were nonstop with good conversation. Lunch lasted for over two hours and could have continued longer, but Cindi had to get to the hospital. I felt that all of us were reluctant to get up and leave for fear that this magical day would end. I know that I was, and I know that I will cherish this day and new-found family forever. We said our good-byes, but not before Cindy told me she could understand why her brother loved me so. I was close to tears by now, and could only think, *There is no greater love for man, than to lay down his life for his friend.*

Greater love hath no man than this, that a man lay
down his life for his friends. (John 15:13–17)

Cindy and Bob walking past the Vietnam wall

We parted ways to reflect on the day's events and new relationships. I left with a new purpose and a lighter heart. I truly had come full circle, and Cindy played a major part in that. This gracious, loving lady, with her southern charm, had lifted a burden I'd been carrying for all these years. She is her brother's sister. Some may think this is all coincidence, his dying on June 27, 1967, while taking my place on patrol, and his sister, Cindy, and I would meet for the first time on June 27, 2017, fifty years later. Both of us received some healing on this day, and I prefer to think there was a higher power at work. Cindy has been a godsend for me and her words a great comfort. I can only hope that I've been able to comfort her as she has me.

I want you to know that I am proud of my service and wouldn't change a thing. There's a very deep bond between those of us who served and fought together. If there's a message here, I want it to be one of raising awareness of how war affects our soldiers and trying to understand the PTSD and the horrors they experienced. To my brothers, "Welcome home." Hang in there. It's worth it, and if the country ever has the need for an old soldier, I'll be there along with a bunch of gray-haired old men who feel the same as I when it comes to defending this country.

Sonny, Mom, and Bob after Bob's arrival home

CERTIFICATE OF APPRECIATION

FOR SERVICE IN THE ARMED FORCES OF THE UNITED STATES

ROBERT L GOFF   STAFF SERGEANT E-6   ARMY 30 SEP 1964 - 1 JUL 1970

I extend to you my personal thanks and the sincere appreciation of a grateful nation for your contribution of honorable service to our country. You have helped maintain the security of the nation during a critical time in its history with a devotion to duty and a spirit of sacrifice in keeping with the proud tradition of the military service.

I trust that in the coming years you will maintain an active interest in the Armed Forces and the purpose for which you served.

My best wishes to you for happiness and success in the future.

Richard Nixon

COMMANDER IN CHIEF

Honorable Discharge

from the Armed Forces of the United States of America

This is to certify that

ROBERT LEE GOFF RA 16 776 244 (316 48 1633) STAFF SERGEANT E-6 MILITARY POLICE CORPS REGULAR ARMY

was Honorably Discharged from the

United States Army

on the 1st *day of* JULY 1970 *This certificate is awarded as a testimonial of Honest and Faithful Service*

J. K. Edwards

J. K. EDWARDS
2LT, AGC

CPSIA information can be obtained
at www.ICGtesting.com
Printed in the USA
LVHW092300210120
644374LV00001B/196